EDITOR: MARTIN WINDROW

OSPREY
MILITARY

MEN-AT-ARMS SERIES

163

THE AMERICAN PLAINS INDIANS

First published in Great Britain in 1985 by
Osprey, an imprint of Reed Consumer Books Limited,
Michelin House, 81 Fulham Road,
London SW3 6RB
and Auckland, Melbourne, Singapore and Toronto

Reprinted 1985, 1986, 1987, 1988, 1989, 1991 (twice),
1992, 1994

British Library Cataloguing in Publication Data

Hook, Jason
    The American Plains Indians.—(Men-at-arms
series; 163)
    1. Indians of North America—Great Plains
I. Title   II. Series
970.004'97   E78.G73

ISBN 0-85045-608-8

Filmset in Great Britain
Printed in Hong Kong

This book is dedicated to the late
Edward H. Blackmore.

Acknowledgements
The author and illustrator wish to record their
gratitude for the assistance of Chikala and Penny
Cockerton; Badger and Dawn Kirby; Robin May;
Moose and Lizzie Wells; Ian M. West; Pikey and
Carole Whiteway-Roberts; the Historical Museum,
Berne, Switzerland; and the Museum of Mankind,
London.

Introduction

The central plains of North America, to the east of the Rocky Mountains, provided the homeland for the Plains Indians; here the hunting grounds of the twelve 'typical' tribes coincided with the grazing range of the largest of the buffalo herds. These tribes all shared the common features of extensive use of the tipi, buffalo and horse; the division of warriors into societies; and the religious ceremony called the Sun Dance. Cultural characteristics naturally varied from tribe to tribe, most obviously between the least associated tribes such as the Blackfoot to the north and the southerly Comanche. The Plains tribes inevitably had links with their neighbouring tribes on the borders of the Plains. To the west were the Plateau tribes, such as the Nez Percé; and the south-west desert tribes, such as the Apaches, had originally been among the earliest inhabitants of the Plains. They, like the village farming tribes on the borders of the eastern woodlands, because of their close proximity to the Plains Indians shared with them a number of cultural traits, and in fact occasionally ventured out on to the open grasslands themselves.

The Plains Indians established themselves during a period which is referred to as 'dog-days', because the dog provided their only beast of burden. Most tribes initially ventured west from the eastern woodlands, across the prairies and on to the Plains. However, these pedestrian Indians were unable fully to exploit this hostile environment until after the introduction of the horse, which, by allowing the successful hunting of the buffalo and the adoption of a fully nomadic life, encouraged many tribes to abandon border areas for the central Plains. The adoption of a horse culture heralded the golden age of the Plains Indians—an age abruptly ended by the intervention of the white man, who forced them from their vast homelands into reservations in the second half of the 19th century.

The transitional period of movement on to the open Plains occurred in most cases during the 17th century, although the previously mentioned tribal variations make exact dating impossible. Similarly, while certain characteristics can be considered typical of the Plains Indians as a whole, it is important to note that there were usually variations, both from tribe to tribe and between individuals. Indeed, their society was highly individualistic, partly because they were a very spiritual people. Their life was not centred on physical survival, but on spiritual renewal, and much of it focused on maintaining harmony with the Sacred Powers. The word 'medicine' has come

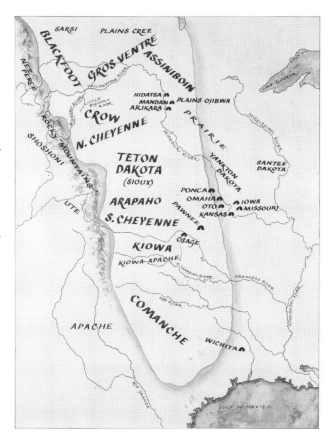

Map showing historic location of the Plains tribes, indicated here in large capitals. Sedentary 'village' tribes are indicated by the earth lodge symbol.

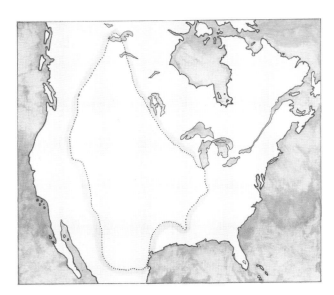

Map showing distribution of the buffalo herds, c.1800—compare with tribal map.

the other side of this tragic but inevitable clash of cultures.)

Community Structure and Camp Life

The divisions of the Plains Indians were far more complex than simply those between tribes. Each tribe was closely related to a number of others linguistically, from the time before movement on to the Plains began. There were also more distinct tribal divisions, and subsequent ramifications into sub-tribes, hunting bands and clans.

The Sioux nation, for example, was initially divided into three separate entities over a period of time: the Dakotas, or Santee Sioux; the Nakotas, or Yankton Sioux; and the Lakotas. While the first two tribes remained on the eastern edge of the Plains, the Lakotas or Teton Sioux migrated west to the central Plains, and became known as the Western Sioux. The Assiniboin tribe were also an off-shoot from the Yankton Sioux, following a later dispute.

Although the number fluctuated slightly as divisions disbanded or united, there were strictly seven sub-tribes of the Teton Sioux, this number being considered integral to the nation's structure. These were the Brulé, Hunkpapa, Miniconjou, Oglala, Oohenonpah, Sans Arcs and Sihasapa.

Even these sub-tribes still contained too many people to be practical units outside the summer months. Just as the summer buffalo herds dispersed into small groups as the grass became less plentiful, so the Plains tribes divided up into compact hunting bands. These were small enough to be mobile and to require only a limited amount of food and grazing, while remaining large enough to defend themselves and to co-operate as a unit, for instance when hunting buffalo. The bands, comprising approximately 20 to 30 families in the case of the Blackfoot, were identified by nicknames. The Oglala Sioux, for example, were divided at one time into six hunting bands or 'tiyopses': the Oglala, Red Water, Old Skin Necklace, Nightcloud, Red Lodge and Short Hair.

The hunting band was the basic working unit for most of the year, until the whole tribe gathered for

to describe the supernatural or spiritual power which the Indians personally received from their deities, and which guided them in hunting, war, healing, and all the other concerns of everyday life.

As a nomadic people their borders were vague, and—in contrast to the men who forced them from it—the Plains Indians had no conception of actually owning the sacred Mother Earth.

Given the special and integrated nature of Indian life and attitudes, it is inevitable that this short study of their culture departs somewhat from the normal Men-at-Arms format. The Plains Indians had no specifically military organisation in the European sense. Their approach to warfare is described in the pages which follow, but only as one aspect of their overall nature. The greater part of Plains Indian history must be seen against a background of constant small-scale warfare between tribes and smaller groups. Their confrontations with the blue-coated soldiers who finally destroyed their independent existence occupied only a few decades, and were not typical of the Indian experience. Those final years demonstrated vividly the enormous gulf which lay between Indian and white attitudes to warfare; and there is a danger of slipping into misleading generalisations if we attempt to analyse the Indian experience through the distorting perspective of the white man's military culture and assumptions. (A future book in this series—*The US Cavalry on the Plains, 1850–90*, by Philip Katcher, planned for publication later in 1985—will describe the summer's hunts and ceremonies. While its size fluctuated to some degree, since members were generally free to move to a more successful band, each unit was comprised mainly of relatives by blood or marriage, a practice which obviously encouraged group unity. This was taken to a greater degree in some tribes by the establishment of clans, whereby affiliation was fixed either patri-locally or matrilocally. The exogamous nature of most bands and clans also served to prevent marriage between relatives, a practice of whose dangers the Indians were keenly aware.

Harmony within the individual hunting bands and in the tribe as a whole was maintained by a number of 'chiefs'. The tribe was considered to be one large family, the camp circle symbolising the family tipi, and the chiefs were at its head. While the structure of each tribe's authorities was complex, the most general distinction between leaders was that between war chief and civil chief. The civil chiefs were generally senior, older men, concerned with the day to day life of the tribe; while war chiefs—the officers of the warrior societies—were vigorously involved in martial affairs. Rôles of authority also extended to groups of respected elders; and to shamans—both in their own right, as for instance when directing the search for buffalo, and as recognised chiefs.

The idea of the Plains Indian chiefs as autocrats is mythical. The many leaders of each tribe held rôles of varying titular superiority, but all enjoyed only limited authority. Even if one band's chief was recognised as the tribe's head man, his rôle would simply be to chair the tribal council. The leaders of the hunting bands would act only in an advisory capacity, so that their authority was only as great as their personal influence. A poor chief would soon lose his position, while the band of a popular leader would prosper and expand. Consequently, to become a chief a man had to display all the virtues expected of a good man. Ideally this meant that anyone could become a chief through leading an exemplary life, although in reality opportunity was sometimes greater for the son of an established leader.

Inspired by the prestige of their elders, young men were certainly keen to follow the path to chieftainship, which lay initially through acquiring the status necessary to lead war parties. A

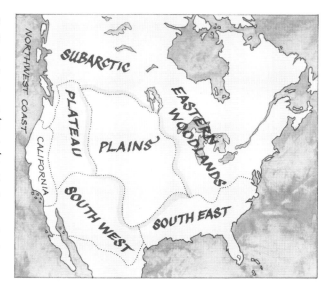

The main cultural divisions of the North American Indians.

recognised warrior could attain advantages in council, both in when he spoke and how much heed was paid to his word. By displaying the other virtues expected of a chief—good sense, honesty, even temper, personal responsibility and unceasing generosity—an aspiring leader set a good example, placed others in his debt, and slowly increased his influence. Since they clearly had to lead by example, the Indians stated that their chiefs were not elected but 'just got that way'.

Important tribal matters were discussed and resolved by the council, one of the most advanced of which was the Council of Forty-Four of the Cheyenne. This comprised 40 chiefs drawn from the ten bands and four Old Man Chiefs, and was guided by a set of regulations (forbidding, for example, the killing of one Cheyenne by another). The council, which met in summer to make decisions for the tribe, represented a strict democracy; working closely with the men's societies, and recognising the wishes of the people, it only made decisions which could be supported by the majority of the tribe.

Since a chief's authority was really only paternal, a good deal of personal responsibility was demanded from each individual. Usually a destructive member of the community was initially reasoned with rather than reprimanded, and there was ample incentive for everyone to make their contribution. Firstly, correct behaviour was instilled into youngsters by the example of the proud, honoured chiefs and warriors. Secondly, the survival of the hunting band was dependent on a co-operative effort, and the obligation was increased by the fact that every member was surrounded by so many close kin. Indeed, the necessity for a band to be able to assign tasks and pool resources promoted the idea that it was good to increase your number of relatives. The convention of treating even quite distant members of the extended family as immediate relatives also fostered unity, and generally ensured that no one was left destitute.

The obligation to marry into a different band helped to maintain the various elements of the tribe as a whole. Whether the man or the woman moved to join the band of their in-laws, the bands were drawn together by blood, and the tribal camp in the summer was eagerly awaited as an annual reunion.

An individual's behaviour was also kept in check in more direct ways, particularly by the importance placed upon public opinion. His standing in relation to his fellow tribal members was central to the Indian's philosophy. Accordingly, while great prestige awaited the virtuous man, ostracism was the punishment of selfishness, cowardice, laziness or dishonesty. The Blackfoot apparently subjected deviants to such public mockery and abuse as to sometimes drive them into exile or on to the war-path; while the Crow formalised such punishment by the recognition of 'joking relatives', who as well as bantering with each other were also expected to shame one another out of deviations in conduct. If such warnings as these, or those from a headman, went unheeded, the council were empowered to exile a man, or to sanction a warrior society to punish him, for instance by destroying his lodge and possessions.

The Tipi

The lodge or 'tipi' provided shelter for all the tribes of the Plains; even the more static village tribes such as the Hidatsa, Mandan and Arikara employed them when they travelled away from their earth lodges. It remains one of the best designed tents in the world today, and was admirably suited to life on the Plains.

The tipi was basically a tilted cone, comprising three or four main poles strapped together at the top with sinew, interspersed with lighter, strengthening poles, and covered with dressed buffalo skins. The lower quarter also had a draught-excluding buffalo-hide liner on the inside, and a narrow entrance facing east was covered with a skin flap.

The main asset of the tipi was its mobility. It could be transported easily, the poles presenting the greatest encumbrance; and with the advent of the horse it became practical to expand it to an average 15 ft base diameter, when it required only two or three horses to drag the poles and carry the lodge-cover. The tipi could be dismantled or erected quickly by two experienced women, and the protection it afforded was excellent. It was sturdy enough to endure the harshest winters, being waterproof and streamlined against the wind, and could be patched easily if damaged. At the top were two smoke-flaps or 'ears', each positioned by an outer pole. These ingenious yet simple devices could be positioned according to the direction and strength of the wind, preventing draughts and allowing free exit of smoke from a central fire, and thus ensuring warmth in winter. The evacuation of smoke was improved by the air currents formed between the outer cover and inner liner, and by the slight tilt of the tipi. The more acute angle of the front of the tipi also braced it against the vicious west winds of the Plains, while the smoke-flaps could be closed to allow rain to run down the outer walls. In the heat of summer the side of the tipi could be rolled up to allow ventilation.

The tipi was considered to be more than just a shelter, however, since it embodied the sacred circular form, and was seen as symbolic of the Indian's world. The painting of visionary ex-

The outside of a painted tipi; and the internal arrangements: (A) Smoke flap (B) Lodge pins (C) Smoke flap pole (D) Door flap (E) Beds (F) Fire (G) Firewood (H) Lifting pole.

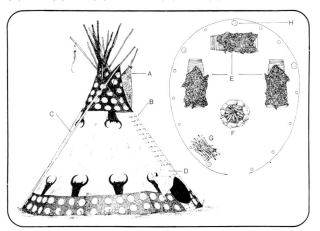

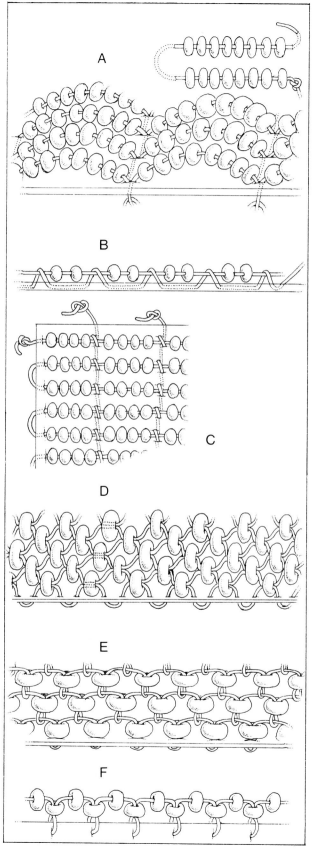

periences and war exploits on the lodge cover, door and liner was common, and made the construction of a new lodge and transfer from the old one a complex ritual.

The Plains Indians managed to live very comfortably in what we would consider cramped conditions, by enforcing strict but subtle etiquette within the tipi; walking between someone else and the central fire, for example, was thought improper. The Indians astonished some white visitors by their apparent freedom yet lack of antagonism within the lodge.

Camp Life

While it would be incorrect to see the wives of most Plains Indian men as mere chattels—and indeed, many women enjoyed a higher status than is often assumed—their society was dominated by the males. This said, however, both sexes had their own important parts to play in the prosperity and survival of the family, band, and tribe.

The men enjoyed greater sexual freedom than the women, and indeed boasted of their exploits, particularly those with married women. The chastity of a woman was greatly valued, however, particularly among the Cheyenne, where 'she who had yielded was disgraced forever'. A noticeably promiscuous girl's marriage prospects were very poor, while virtuous women attracted respected husbands and commanded prestigious rôles in religious ceremonies. Conversely, a prospective Tree-Notcher in the Crow Sun Dance who was not genuinely chaste had to decline the honour by declaring, 'My moccasin has a hole in it'.

Courtship was accordingly formalised to a degree, and young couples had to be wary of being seen together. Some boys made approaches when a girl went to fetch water or as she wandered with a friend through camp, but she was not often far from her grandmother's watchful eye. If a girl's parents considered her ready for marriage, they might discreetly let it be known that suitors could

Methods of beadwork: (A) Lazy stitch; covers large areas with bands of parallel rows sewn down at the ends; eight to ten beads in a row. (B) Overlaid or 'spot' stitch; two threads, one for the beads, one to attach them to the cloth; used for gently curved lines. (C) Crow stitch; rows of threaded beads secured by a second thread at right angles. (D) Netted stitch, 'gourd'; using the bead as a knot. (E) Netted stitch, 'brick'; using the looped thread as a knot. (F) Edge-beading, 'one up, one down'; many variations on this were used to edge areas of beadwork.

7

Some of the finest examples of Plains Indian beadwork are seen on moccasins. This pair are decorated with 'lazy stitch' beading in red, white, green and dark blue, the edges finished with looped trimming. Hunkpapa Sioux, collected at Fort Randall, South Dakota, 1870–80. (Berne Historical Museum)

approach. It was considered proper among many tribes for young men to cover their heads with 'courting blankets' to conceal their identity when they met the girl outside her tipi, where they embraced her with the blanket, allowing private but respectable conversation. Love-medicines and flutes also played their parts in the rituals of courting, invoking the power of animals such as the elk to inspire the faint-hearted, and to render chosen girls helpless with love.

If a suitor was encouraged by a young woman, and if his family sanctioned the match, then they would help him gather together gifts which an intermediary would take to the girl's lodge. If her family approved, they would take gifts of an equivalent value along with the bride to the boy's lodge; if not, they simply returned the original gifts. In the event of a marriage being agreed, a feast or simple ceremony set the seal on the proceedings. This was considered the honourable way to marry, although elopements were not uncommon between couples who faced opposition from their families.

Just as the relatives secured the marriage by exchanging gifts, so it was seen as a bond between families rather than simply between two in-dividuals. Indeed, the exchange of gifts might continue for many years. One of the newly married

couple would move to the other's hunting band, and was regarded as a replacement for those members of the family unit who had themselves married into a different band. Hence the husband, in a matrilocal society, would become a member of a new unit, and would be welcomed as another provider of food and protection.

Marriage also brought taboos between the couple and their respective in-laws, usually as a sign of respect. Even before marriage, brothers and sisters were commonly kept apart from each other after a certain age despite, or perhaps because of, their closeness. After marriage, this extended to a man and his father-in-law or mother-in-law, to the extent that they were often tabooed from even looking at each other. Conversely, brothers and sisters-in-law were usually permitted a very free relationship.

A man's relations with his sister-in-law might indeed go further, since in polygamous marriages, which were quite common among many tribes, the wives were frequently sisters. A man was often considered to be under obligation to take care of his sisters-in-law if they were widowed; he might be offered his wife's sisters as wives, or might choose to ask them, since having sisters as plural wives was considered to minimise any jealousy.

Polygamy had very practical advantages for the Plains Indians. Firstly, because of the nature of this

Another fine pair of beaded moccasins, probably of Gros Ventre workmanship. (British Museum)

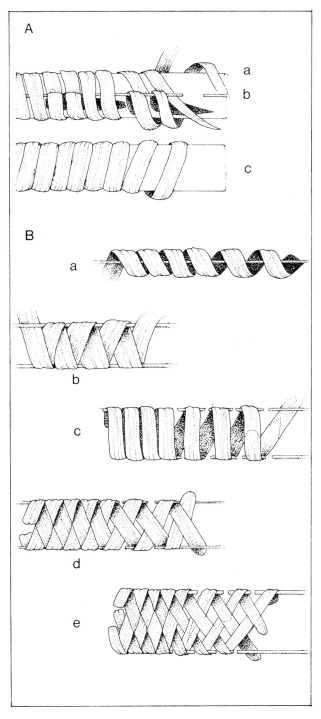

Methods of quillwork:
(**A**) *Wrapping with quills:* (**a**) **Back** (**b**) **Sinew thread which holds quill ends** (**c**) **Front.**
(**B**) *Plaiting with quills:* (**a**) **One thread and one quill sewing, creating straight or curved lines.** (**b**) **Two thread and one quill sewing, crossed sewing forming triangles.** (**c**) **Two thread and one quill straight sewing—dotted line shows how a new quill was worked in.** (**d**) **Two thread and two quill plaiting or sewing, forming small diamonds down the centre.** (**e**) **Two thread and three quill plaiting.**

warlike society, the women far outnumbered the men. To increase the population efficiently, and to replace lost warriors, polygamous marriage gave every woman an opportunity to raise children. Secondly, the chores of a prominent man's wife were arduous, and while a second wife could help maintain the lodge and prepare meals for her husband and his associates, she also provided company for the first wife while he was at war. The first wife would remain as the head of the household—she was called the 'sits-beside-me-wife' by the Blackfoot—and she would suffer no disgrace from her husband's subsequent marriages; indeed, she might even put forward the idea. For the men, plural marriage provided the potential to amass more property, since extra wives could prepare many more robes for trade, which more than compensated for the need to secure more food.

Men's and women's responsibilities and chores were clearly divided. The women, as well as raising children, were responsible for maintaining and organising the lodge, transporting it, and keeping the inside tidy. A man's wife could also be expected to help butcher the meat he had secured, to prepare his meals, and to ensure his comfort. The dressing of skins—an arduous process involving cleaning, curing, scraping and tanning of very heavy hides—again fell to the women who, moreover, had then to convert them into usable articles. Women were responsible for the intricate crafts of quilling and beading; beadwork, encouraged by the availability of trade beads, became more popular after 1830. The quality of these painstaking, decorative crafts can be seen in many artefacts such as moccasins, pipe-bags, cradles, and dresses. Proficiency in quilling and beading, and indeed in daily chores, was the women's equivalent of the men's deeds on the warpath. There were women's guilds comparable to the men's societies, such as the Quillers' Society, and prominent craftswomen attained prestige on a par with that of successful warriors.

The men's primary rôles were to feed and protect their families; and if the women's chores were more laborious, the men's were more dangerous.

The contrasting male and female rôles were developed from childhood, and children often mimicked the lives of their parents. Young girls were often given miniature tipis and dolls to look after, and imitated such things as the Scalp Dance,

Quilled deerskin shirt of Blackfoot workmanship, decorated with red and white quillwork, painted symbols and ermine fur. (British Museum)

being taught the crafts necessary for a good wife in their teens. Boys were taught to hunt and fight, and were toughened up in preparation for the fiercely competitive warrior's life that awaited nearly all of them. They were steeled for combat with vicious wrestling games, and taught the virtues of courage, while their endurance, riding and shooting skills were developed through games and guidance. Between 11 and 15 years of age they would progress from chasing calves to hunting in earnest. Finally, they would act as water-carriers in their first war-party, thus confirming the attainment of adulthood.

Hunting and the Horse

Since the Plains tribes had generally abandoned the static farming life in favour of roaming the Plains in search of game, hunting naturally formed a vital part of their lives. Even the village tribes such as the Ponca and Mandan, who subsisted mainly on their own crops, relied on the buffalo to provide meat in the summer months. Although the true nomads supplemented their diet with vegetables and berries, the bulk of their food came from hunting a wide variety of animals. Game such as the antelope and deer provided varied meat and skins; the beaver and weasel were sought for their prized fur; and birds were killed for their feathers.

Kiowa woman and baby, 1890s; the dress, moccasins and cradleboard are all typical of this southern Plains tribe. She is identified by Mayhall (see Bibliography) as Yea-Gyo-Taup, mother of Homer Buffalo.

Unquestionably, though, the staff of life for the Plains Indian was the buffalo, which was regarded as constant proof of the benevolence of the Sacred Powers. They were not only plentiful, roaming the Plains in herds of millions stretching over many miles, but also provided the Indians with more than just food. The tribes ingeniously and gratefully made use of every part of the buffalo (see accompanying diagram) to the extent that it supplied an incredible proportion of their basic needs, providing clothing, tools, shelter, fuel and food.

As the life-sustaining force, and patron of such virtues as strength and fertility, the revered buffalo was a central feature of religion. Mediums such as buffalo skulls, curiously shaped 'buffalo stones', and names derived from the animal (such as Sitting Bull) all invoked its sacred power.

Ritual also surrounded the hunting of the buffalo, with songs, dances and ceremonies assuring the successful renewal of the herds each year. One simple practice was to leave the hearts of butchered animals on the plain after a hunt, in the belief that they would replenish the herd with new life. Other ceremonies, such as the Mandan Bull Dance, symbolised the procreation of each year's calves.

Those shamans who possessed medicine derived from visions of the buffalo would be responsible for ensuring that their patron animals approached the camp. They would use their power, along with special regalia such as buffalo hoof rattles or skulls, to call the large herds to the area at times when their return was anticipated or when food was scarce. Supernatural power also extended to the actual killing of the buffalo, the appropriate shamans undergoing rituals to ensure the success of a hunt.

Various techniques were used to hunt buffalo, depending upon the time of year, and evolving with the use of the horse. Individuals or small groups sought buffalo when the hunting regulations permitted. Their prey always had to be approached from downwind, since buffalo have an acute sense of smell to compensate for their poor vision and hearing. Disguises such as wolf-skins enabled a pedestrian hunter to approach very close to a herd. The bow and arrow's silence explained its general preference over firearms, since the herd were not necessarily alarmed immediately a shot was loosed. By hunting in small groups, the hunters were also able to head off the buffaloes' retreat. In the deep snows of winter hunters on foot, sometimes using snowshoes, could drive buffalo into drifts or on to ice where their weight of up to 2,000 lbs rendered them helpless. This particular technique survived the coming of the horse, while the speed of a mounted hunter over relatively snow-free ground led to the adaption of the other individual methods of hunting.

The only way to secure a large amount of meat was through a co-operative effort. The communal drive or 'piskin' was the oldest form of group hunting, and employed all the able members of a band. The principle was to lure or drive a herd towards a corral or precipice by mimicking a calf, by enticing the leading animals, by using medicine or by sending runners behind the buffalo. The members of the band would form a long 'V', hiding themselves behind rocks or makeshift fences converging on the enclosure or escarpment. As the buffalo passed them these people leapt from hiding and began waving and screaming, spooking the herd and causing them to stampede, hopefully towards the trap. As each one leapt out the path available to the buffalo narrowed, until they realised the danger. As the leading buffalo strained to stop, they would be driven into the stockade or hurled over the cliff by the momentum of the blindly charging bulk of the herd, who would themselves have no time to stop. The stockade's entrance was usually a sharp drop or an iced-over

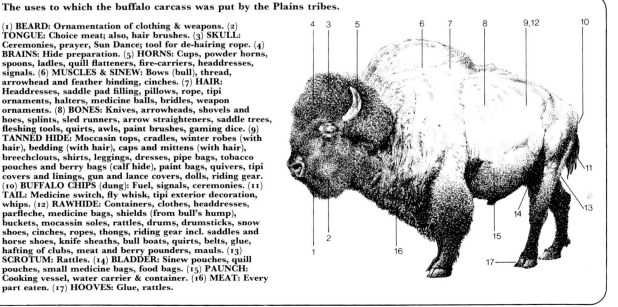

The uses to which the buffalo carcass was put by the Plains tribes.

(1) **BEARD:** Ornamentation of clothing & weapons. (2) **TONGUE:** Choice meat; also, hair brushes. (3) **SKULL:** Ceremonies, prayer, Sun Dance; tool for de-hairing rope. (4) **BRAINS:** Hide preparation. (5) **HORNS:** Cups, powder horns, spoons, ladles, quill flatteners, fire-carriers, headdresses, signals. (6) **MUSCLES & SINEW:** Bows (bull), thread, arrowhead and feather binding, cinches. (7) **HAIR:** Headdresses, saddle pad filling, pillows, rope, tipi ornaments, halters, medicine balls, bridles, weapon ornaments. (8) **BONES:** Knives, arrowheads, shovels and hoes, splints, sled runners, arrow straighteners, saddle trees, fleshing tools, quirts, awls, paint brushes, gaming dice. (9) **TANNED HIDE:** Moccasin tops, cradles, winter robes (with hair), bedding (with hair), caps and mittens (with hair), breechclouts, shirts, leggings, dresses, pipe bags, tobacco pouches and berry bags (calf hide), paint bags, quivers, tipi covers and linings, gun and lance covers, dolls, riding gear. (10) **BUFFALO CHIPS** (dung): Fuel, signals, ceremonies. (11) **TAIL:** Medicine switch, fly whisk, tipi exterior decoration, whips. (12) **RAWHIDE:** Containers, clothes, headdresses, parfleche, medicine bags, shields (from bull's hump), buckets, mocassin soles, rattles, drums, drumsticks, snow shoes, cinches, ropes, thongs, riding gear incl. saddles and horse shoes, knife sheaths, bull boats, quirts, belts, glue, hafting of clubs, meat and berry pounders, mauls. (13) **SCROTUM:** Rattles. (14) **BLADDER:** Sinew pouches, quill pouches, small medicine bags, food bags. (15) **PAUNCH:** Cooking vessel, water carrier & container. (16) **MEAT:** Every part eaten. (17) **HOOVES:** Glue, rattles.

slope, preventing the buffalo from escaping the waiting hunters, while those driven over an escarpment would be killed or crippled by the fall.

The piskin was an ingenious method of compensating for the Indians' lack of mobility in pre-horse days, and could provide a huge amount of meat in return for a brief, if arduous and hazardous effort. It was unreliable, however, since the buffalo might simply never approach the area (particularly if the smell of a previous slaughter still lingered), or might suddenly veer away from the trap. It was a way of using group co-operation, and the meat was divided amongst the whole band; but its deficiencies led to the decline of the communal drive once horses became available, and only tribes poor in horses, such as the Plains Cree and Assiniboin, continued to rely on it. Most tribes evolved methods which used more fully the skills of mounted hunters, and were therefore more popular and indeed more successful.

The 'surround', which also stemmed from pre-horse days, became much easier with the advent of the horse. The principle, whether on foot or horseback, was to approach the buffalo in two lines or an arc, and then to converge on them by joining up into a wide circle and tightening it like a noose. The rather stupid animals became confused, and

The arrangement of the Cheyenne camp circle. (After Wissler)

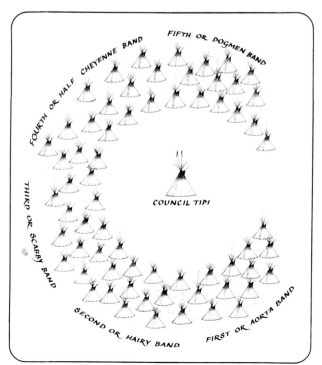

FIFTH OR DOGMEN BAND
FOURTH OR HALF CHEYENNE BAND
THIRD OR SCABBY BAND
COUNCIL TIPI
SECOND OR HAIRY BAND
FIRST OR AORTA BAND

the leading buffalo would turn away from the screaming hunters and either run in circles or charge back into the centre of the herd, goring each other. The milling mass could be picked off with arrows and lances; and although the buffalo would frequently kill or injure some of the hunters, the crowding caused by the 'surround' reduced their battering-ram power, and made possible the slaughter of a large number of animals. While the 'surround' was much more practicable and efficient on horseback, it was not feasible in certain terrain, and still failed to make the best use of the horse.

The 'chase' employed the Plains riders' exceptional skills to the full. It was a straight mounted rush by the hunters from downwind of the buffalo, who would turn and flee when they realised the danger, spreading out as they ran. The cows were followed by the bulls, with the calves bringing up the rear. Unlike the 'surround', the chase made full use of the mobility of a rider, since he was free to select each individual quarry, closing on and evading the galloping buffalo as he judged best and as his skill allowed.

Once a herd had been located, the hunters approached as near as possible without disturbing the buffalo; then mounted their 'buffalo-runners', leaving common mounts with the women and children. Buffalo-runners were agile, swift and courageous horses, highly prized by their riders, and trained specifically for riding close in to the buffalo without flinching, guided only by the pressure of their rider's knees. A man's ability in the chase was only as good as his buffalo-runner, and he used this horse for nothing else.

The mounted hunters lined up equidistant from the herd, allowing all an equal opportunity, preventing individuals from scattering the herd prematurely, and ensuring the largest possible kill. At a signal the hunters charged, the superior buffalo-runners running down the cows if they were prime. As a hunter closed on his chosen target his mount brought him to the right rear flank of the buffalo in the case of a right-handed bowman, or to the left if he was a lancer. When he was as close as possible the rider released his already-nocked arrow, aiming behind the last rib of the buffalo to hit the vitals and shooting with great force, since a weak or misplaced arrow would not stop its powerful target. While some hunters employed the lance, firearms were not very effective before repeating rifles were introduced, since only these could compete with the rapid discharge accomplished by the bowman.

At the sound of the bow string, the buffalo-runner would veer away from the buffalo to evade its horns. The horse then kept pace if, as was quite common, further shots were required to complete the kill. Then the hunter would select another buffalo, repeating the process until his horse tired and the remnants of the herd outdistanced him. On average a competent man could kill two buffalo, only the supreme hunters boasting four or five of the choicest beasts.

A further advantage of using the bow was that every hunter could identify his own arrows, and claim the meat that he had killed. So, while the hunt was still a communal one, it promoted individual achievement and appealed to the Indian's competitive nature, both between hunters and in the deadly contest between man and beast.

Both men and women took part in butchering, depending upon the tribe. Animals were heavily butchered when practical and necessary, and the

bulk of the meat taken back to the camp on packhorses. Raw meat was also eagerly devoured on the spot; raw liver, for example, was sometimes eaten still hot and dripping blood.

The chase naturally had its dangers, both in the possibility of a horse stumbling, and of a buffalo turning and hooking with its horns. With the increasing reliance on the horse, however, many tribes favoured this method of hunting, since it ensured that the better the combined skills of mount and rider, the greater the chance of escaping injury.

The size of a band, the distance it had to travel and its hunting methods were dictated by the availability, movement and quality of the buffalo's meat and coat. Accordingly, the life of the nomadic Indians varied with the four seasons.

During autumn, from about August to November, the tribes were dispersed into their individual bands. A band moved camp when lack of game drove them on, until their designated winter village

A northern Plains camp scene, probably Assiniboin. Of special interest is the travois and horse furniture. The travois was an essential means of transporting goods, children, or even sick adults; it was originally hauled by dogs in the pre-horse era.

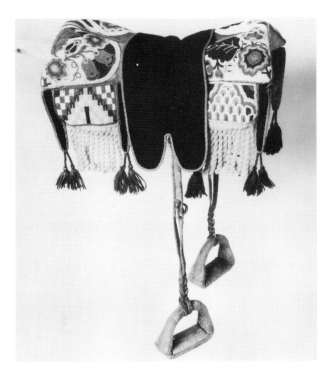

Beautifully beaded example of a saddle; museum-listed as Blackfoot, it could just as easily be Plains Cree or Chippewa. The naturalism of the motifs in the design casts doubt upon the Blackfoot identification. (British Museum)

site was reached. Individual hunting provided fresh meat throughout autumn, and around October communal hunts—usually drives until the later days—were employed to build up winter reserves from the fattened buffalo. Until the bad weather set in, the camp spent the late autumn in preparing dried meat and in obtaining and dressing hides, originally for their own lodges and clothes but in later days to supply the white traders.

During the winter months the bands sought shelter from the bitter, open Plains, and established static camps far enough apart not to deprive each other of game. Camp was only moved if a band faced starvation or needed fresh pasture, and then only if the move could be completed by nightfall. The severe weather and scarcity of buffalo, likewise dispersed into small groups seeking shelter, restricted hunting considerably. Individuals and small groups sought buffalo when the weather allowed, to supplement the dried meat supplies which were so vital when conditions confined the Indians to their lodges. The village sites were often situated near communal drives, in hope of obtaining not only precious meat, but also the shaggy winter coats of the buffalo—ideal for robes,

which were in great demand until the white man's trading season ended in about April.

When better weather heralded the arrival of spring, the bands eagerly followed the buffalo back out on to the open Plains. The richer grass ensured a plentiful supply of meat, which was generally hunted on a family basis. Communal hunts were organised when opportune; as the bands moved with the buffalo herds, so their paths crossed, so that two or three might unite in one large camp.

The only time the entire tribe or sub-tribe gathered, other than for tribal defence, was during the summer months. The bands drifted together until they were united in one spectacular camp circle; in its purest form this had the bands camped in a fixed order, as among the Cheyenne (see diagram). The summer camp was a time for reunions, affirmation of tribal unity, important councils and religious ceremonies.

While the whole tribe was together the selected warrior societies would enforce the hunt regulations, forbidding anyone to chase game outside of the communal hunts, since individuals might alert the larger herds. These regulations were very important, for although the buffalo were plentiful the tribal leaders were responsible for feeding many mouths.

The tribal hunts in the summer usually took the form of the 'surround' or the chase, and as well as food, the hunt was expected to yield sufficient tongues for the ceremonies of the Sun Dance. After the Sun Dance's conclusion, and often after a final communal hunt, the tribe would once again divide up and begin the journey towards and preparation for their winter camps.

Trade

One important offshoot from hunting was trade, both between tribes and with the whites; this was particularly so after the establishment of the white man's trading posts, of which there were approximately 150 by 1840.

Inter-tribal trade provided each tribe with variants on their own produce; the true nomads, for instance, were able to obtain maize, beans, squash and tobacco from the village tribes such as the Hidatsa, in exchange for their hunting products. Furthermore, it disseminated a related culture, associated tribes on other terms than those of war, and maintained the sign language with which the various Plains tribes could communicate even if divided by linguistic differences.

It was the trade-goods of the whites, however, which had the more acute effect on the evolution of the Plains Indians. In the 1600s the Spanish settlements in Mexico provided the first horses, while the French and English traders in the northeast began supplying the Indians with primitive firearms; and both were passed on from tribe to tribe.

The effects of the introduction of horses and firearms were dramatic. Firstly, they contributed to the migration of sedentary woodland tribes on to the Plains. In 1650, for example, the Sioux lived in the woodland Milles Lac region bordering the Plains, and only irregularly hunted buffalo. Drawn by the potential of the herds, however, and driven by their enemies the Chippewa and the allied Cree and Assiniboin—all recently supplied with firearms—the Teton Sioux moved south-west,

Pad saddle, seen from above. Made of tanned skin stuffed with deer or buffalo hair, or perhaps grass, it is decorated with quillwork in red, blue, brown, black and white. This piece is probably Sioux, pre-1837; structurally, its resemblance to a Scythian or Altai saddle found in Russia and dating from at least the 4th century BC—the dawn of military horsemanship—is quite remarkable. (Berne Historical Museum)

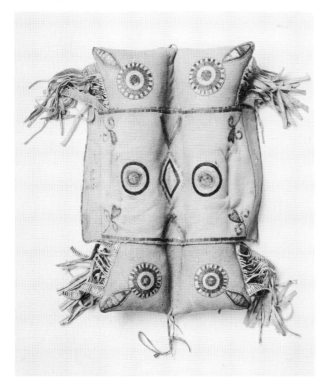

assuming their typical nomadic, buffalo hunting rôle by 1700. By 1750 they had successfully established themselves in territory west of the Missouri River.

Naturally, the life of the nomads was altered radically by the horse, which established their superiority over the sedentary tribes. The whole balance of power between the tribes was altered, while certain tribes established themselves as trading centres.

Fur companies, such as the Hudson's Bay Company established as early as 1670, continued trading with the Indians; items such as beads had a marked effect on their culture, and metal tools and utensils like kettles, knives and arrowheads eased the chores of everyday life. By 1830 the increased demand for buffalo robes meant that for the first time the Indians were—ominously—killing significantly more game than was dictated by their basic needs. Another effect was to make tribes reliant to a certain extent on the white traders, particularly as the only source of ammunition for their guns. However, one trade item which they had acquired had become so independent as to appear indigenous: and that was the horse.

The Horse

From 1600 onwards, the Pueblo Indians who worked on the Spanish ranches of northern Mexico, New Mexico and Texas gained experience in handling horses; and, through friendly contact, they passed on their knowledge to neighbouring Indians such as the Apaches. Through theft, trade, and straying from the open ranches, the horse was gradually acquired by the southernmost Indians of the Plains. The 1680 Pueblo revolt also freed thousands of mounts, and by 1700 they had spread through the Apaches to the Comanche and Kiowa, and west of the Rockies from the Ute up to the Shoshoni. By 1750 the Sioux, Cheyenne, Crow and Blackfoot all had horses, and by 1770 the diffusion was complete.

A tribe's initial reaction to the horse was one of awe, but this gave way to celebration as they realised its potential. Here was an animal with all the uses of the dog magnified by its size and temperament, which was also capable of bearing a man. The Indian names for the horse, such as 'Elk-dog', 'Sacred-dog', and 'God-dog', reflected the regard and sanctity in which they held it, as well as its size and utility.

By extending the size of their hunting grounds, the horse ushered in a period of constant tribal warfare among the Plains Indians; the new mobility of the equestrian tribes led to the repeated ousting of weaker tribes from their territories. Hunting grounds were not usually won through full-scale battles, however, but through constant harassment by raiding parties.

The 'horse raid' was not intended to be a bloody affair, but was undertaken by a small group of warriors who sought to steal the horses of their enemies by stealth. The success of such raiders represented a victory for their tribe, as well as bringing personal prestige—particularly if they escaped with the prized war or buffalo horses which were usually picketed outside their owner's tipi.

While the horse increased the danger of war simply by making war more feasible, it also heralded an age of prosperity for the Plains tribes. Only with such an efficient beast of burden could they embark with any success on a fully nomadic existence. Camp could be moved further and much more quickly, while more equipment now became manageable. Larger lodges, greater food supplies and previously inconceivable luxury items all

A wooden-framed Crow woman's saddle covered with rawhide. The pommel and cantle have a second covering of soft, tanned skin. It is decorated with pendants beaded with white, dull green, rose, and two shades of blue, on red and olive green woollen cloth. (Berne Historical Museum)

illustrated the opportunities for wealth provided by the horse.

Indeed, the horse actually became a measure of wealth, providing material evidence of a man's prestige. The successful warrior could build up a large herd by raiding, and gained influence through the generosity he showed with his horses. Through offering them as loans and gifts the benefactor gained prestige, while the poor man was also helped. This extended to the horse being given as compensation to a wronged man, and to their being offered as gifts accompanying marriage proposals.

Clearly, then, the horse permeated every aspect of the Indians' lives. Trade, culture, leisure, hunting and war all came to revolve around it. Consequently, children were accustomed to horses from an early age; infants were carried in back-cradles while their mothers rode, and both boys and girls were capable riders by the age of seven. The boys then progressed to trick-riding; for example, a Comanche youth learned to ride bareback, and to pick up increasingly heavy weights from the ground at a gallop, in preparation for rescuing fallen comrades. Boys also tended the herds, and at an early age would be responsible for breaking horses—often in a swamp or river to discourage bucking and provide a soft landing! Throughout his life the Indian would be dependent on the horse, which even pervaded his religion. Its importance was such that it followed a prominent man to the grave, being sacrificed to accompany its rider after death as it had during life.

Naturally, the horse had an immeasurable effect on the fighting ability of the Plains Indians. Within a short time they had fully adopted a horse culture, to the extent that Indians such as the Comanche were said to be transformed from ungainliness to grace and elegance simply by mounting a horse. Logically, they also developed into fearsome fighters on horseback, the Sioux being described by Gen. George Crook of the US Army as the greatest light cavalry the world had ever known.

The mounted Indian warriors could taunt pedestrian enemies and outflank apparently superior opposition with their remarkable skills, performing such feats of horsemanship as lifting fallen comrades to the saddle, and concealing themselves by hanging below their mounts while at the gallop. Their affinity with nature and knowledge of animals contributed greatly to their riding ability, superior to that of most whites; and to their immensely skilled fieldcraft, which allowed them to maximise the advantages of mounted mobility.

The horse suited the needs of the Indians so admirably and was used so effectively that it ushered in a whole new culture and lifestyle. By placing them on a much more equal footing with their environment, the horse could be said to have created, rather than just transformed, the Plains Indians.

War

While the material motives of securing favourable camp-sites and hunting grounds, and of capturing horses, contributed to tribal conflict, there were other and less obvious factors underlying the warlike nature of the Plains Indians.

Tribes sought security through aggression and self-assertion. Rather than using large numbers to destroy a weak enemy, they would instead send small war-parties into the heart of their most powerful adversary's territory. By displaying such recklessness a tribe struck at the very spirit of their enemy, while proclaiming their own strength, bravery, and—in particular—faith in their 'medicine'.

Clearly, then, an intrinsic part of war was to demonstrate complete disregard for fear, and this was well illustrated by the way in which the individual warriors fought. The actual killing of an enemy was generally secondary to displays of bravado, the greatest honour being accorded to those men who showed contempt for their adversaries, thus mirroring the tribal motives of asserting strength, superiority and the resolve necessary to survive.

War was consequently the most important sphere in which a man had to prove his worth, and the most direct way of achieving prestige. It was considered a man's business to fight, and the idea that it was 'better to die in battle than of old age or sickness' was instilled at an early age. The courting of danger brought renown, while cowardice met with scorn, and age robbed a man of his vigour and usefulness.

Because of the complex motives behind conflict

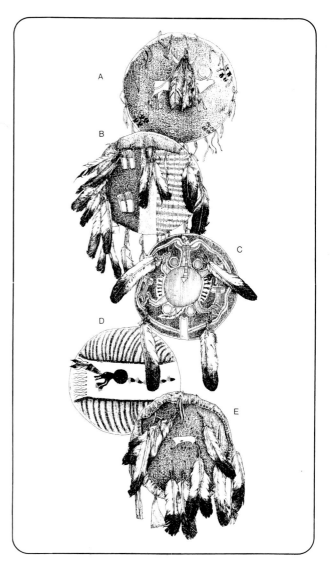

Examples of Plains Indian shields: **(A) Cheyenne; this has a separate cover decorated with cow and moon symbols, hoof prints and feathers. (B) Cheyenne; painted, and decorated with cloth and eagle feathers. (C) Mandan; the painted turtle symbol stems from the owner's vision, and it is embellished with eagle feathers. (D) Crow shield with painted cover. (E) This shield is probably Sioux; it is decorated with a small painting of a bear in green, and with eagle feathers.**

on the Plains, warfare took various forms. Naturally, repelling enemy attacks was one important rôle of a band's warriors, while offensive action was divided into the scalp raid and the horse raid.

Prior to the use of the horse, indecisive clashes between whole tribes exchanging arrows at long range were interspersed with more frequent, destructive attacks on small camps by superior forces. After the introduction of the horse, all raids for scalps became less frequent; while clashes of

These Northern Cheyenne warriors were photographed while working for an early 'Wild West Show' circus. Although such sources must be examined with caution, this seems to illustrate the Plains Indian warrior's costume quite faithfully.

commonest way for a man to display his courage and acquire wealth and prestige, and involved a much smaller raiding party. While the men's departure was again preceded by the invocation of 'medicine', and their successful return was cause for celebration, this was more understated than with the scalp raid, just as the raiders sought horses through silence and stealth rather than in a flamboyant clash with their enemy in a bid for scalps.

The taking of horses was not the only factor effecting a warrior's rise to prominence. While this provided him with material evidence of his exploits, the Indians also had to prove themselves by attaining other war honours or 'coups'.

The coup proper was to deliberately touch an enemy with the hand or something held in the hand—e.g. a weapon, a quirt, or a specifically-designed willow wand called a 'coup-stick'—without actually harming him. The Cheyenne warrior Yellow Nose, for example, gained great honour by snatching Custer's standard at the Little Big Horn, and using it to count coup on the enemy soldiers.

There were many other war honours which were also termed as coups, and rewarded with honorific symbols depicted on the warrior's body, clothes, horse and possessions, signifying status. Different tribes recognised different exploits as war honours, and graded them according to their worth. The Crow gave special recognition to a man who had led

tribal proportions between hundreds of warriors, which had sometimes included men from allied tribes, now became very rare. The scalp raid was usually launched to seek revenge on an enemy tribe, or to conclude a period of mourning. It was a highly organised affair, and consequently involved a considerable amount of ceremony. Before the raiders' departure vows and sacrifices to the Sacred Powers invoked success, while variations on the 'big' or 'horseback' dance—where the warriors donned full war regalia and paraded with their horses—aroused tribal spirit.

If the raiders—usually comprising a number of relatives of the person being mourned—returned successful, the camp would revive the ceremonies with a Scalp or Victory Dance. These dances varied from tribe to tribe, but commonly they were a celebration of the warriors' victory and bravery. Scalps were displayed on poles, often carried by the women of the camp; coups were recited, and a scalp might be presented as a replacement for the avenged camp member, an appeasement for his relatives.

The horse raid was a much more frequent and spontaneous event, often being undertaken without consultation with the band's chiefs. It became the

A Blackfoot war shirt, collected in 1837. It is partly painted dark brown, edged with red ochre, and decorated with a large disc of orange, blue and dark brown quillwork; turquoise and white beadwork; brown human hair, and grey horse hair. Note the bear claw attached to the shoulder. (Berne Historical Museum)

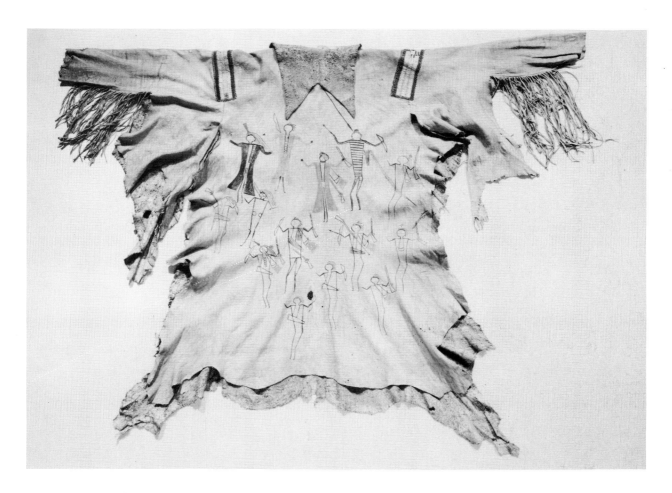

a successful raid, captured a picketed horse, counted coup, and snatched an enemy's gun. This last was considered the ultimate coup by the Blackfoot, who placed it well above the killing of an enemy, which was rated only as a minor coup by many tribes; the Assiniboin who touched a fallen enemy gained more status than the warrior who had shot him.

War exploits were also accorded varying honour depending upon their circumstances. For example, to strike a coup upon an enemy whose prowess was denoted by regalia such as a war-bonnet, or to do so actually within the enemy camp, naturally elevated the deed. Further, the first coup counted in any encounter held the greatest value; while more than one coup could be counted on the same person, the value of each diminished after the 'first coup'. The Arapaho and Sioux permitted four such coups, while the Cheyenne recognised only three.

The rewards of a notable war record were great for the Plains warrior, bringing him the right to wear specific regalia; these displayed his prowess,

A war shirt, probably Sioux, decorated with quilled and beaded bands and brown maidenhair fern. The shirt is painted front and back with stylised human figures in black, red and green. These may possibly represent warriors of other tribes killed by the shirt's owner. It is stained inside and out with red ochre. This piece dates from 1837 at the latest. (Berne Historical Museum)

and thus increased his reputation and influence. (Conversely, it was a humiliating experience for a man to have coups counted upon himself.) A proven warrior was given the honour of reciting his coups, of naming children and piercing their ears, of participating in religious ceremonies, and of progressing through the ranks of his particular warrior society.

The scalp, like a stolen horse or captured gun, also provided an individual with a trophy of war and, as proof of a killing, denoted a coup. While all tribes apart from the Cree and Sioux regarded scalping as subordinate to other coups, it was nevertheless widely practised, since a scalp was a tangible symbol of success. The hair was considered synonymous with an Indian's identity and an extension of his soul, so scalping also spiritually killed a victim. This again reflected the tribal complex of self-assertion, particularly on a vengeance raid: the scalping undermined the soul of the enemy and spiritually replaced and avenged the tribe's own deceased. Scalps were flourished at Scalp Dances, and were sometimes kept thereafter, stretched across wooden hoops and decorated, for example, as powerful war medicines.

Weapons

The Plains Indians naturally possessed a wide variety of weapons, ranging from the indigenous bows, lances and clubs to the firearms and metal-bladed weapons provided by the whites.

The bow remained one of the most popular weapons from the early 'dog-days' throughout the conflict with the whites, and was used with great skill for both hunting and war. It was adapted to suit a mounted bowman by being reduced in length, to only 3 ft in some cases, making it manageable on horseback and lessening the risk of impalement in case of a fall. Bows were occasionally fashioned from horn, but more commonly from wood; this was often strengthened with strips of sinew, which was also the material for the bowstring. The making of any bow was a skilled craft, recurved bows being particularly valued for their power and beauty. Even good, straight arrows were difficult to make, and consequently were also prized. Arrowheads of bone or stone were quickly replaced by iron or steel when these became readily available from traders.

The Plains warrior's use of the bow was on a par with his mastery of the horse, and was also developed from an early age. Arrows were released with great accuracy, and enough power to go clean through a buffalo or a man's skull at close range. The Indians usually tried to close the range. Accurate at 100 yards, the bow was not effective over about 150 yards. (There have been claims for a maximum range of 300 yards under perfect conditions: this would be an astonishing performance for a bow of horseback length unless it was of composite wood/horn/sinew construction, and sharply recurved in shape.) Consequently, because the bow also had the advantages of silence and a rapid rate of discharge, it remained in full use even after the introduction of the gun.

The earliest firearms obtained by the Indians were inaccurate, slow to load and cumbersome; and while they were cheap and sturdy, their main advantages lay in their effectiveness at close range, and the initial shock and fear created by their alien appearance and effect. The typical firearms provided by the fur companies were termed 'North-West' guns, and were made by a variety of manufacturers. They were light, muzzle-loading, single-shot flintlock muskets varying from .50 to .70 in. calibre, with an enlarged trigger guard to allow firing with a mittened hand. The Indians customised their guns, shortening the barrels for ease of use on horseback, adding decoration in the form of brass studs and beautifully beaded buckskin cases, and using rawhide to repair any breakages.

Heavier, more accurate and powerful flintlock and percussion 'trade-rifles' were introduced between 1800 and 1850, but, being muzzle-loaders, these still had a low rate of fire. Consequently, while ownership of a gun was always prestigious, it was only after the 1860s, when repeating breech-loaders began to reach the tribes, that firearms began to supersede the bow. By the late 19th century, however, most warriors possessed either a rifle, such as the treasured 1866 Winchester carbine, or a pistol, the six-shot Civil War Remingtons and Colts making excellent horseback weapons for close combat.

A large number of other weapons were used, all of which were affected by the trade goods of the whites. Stone clubs were the most popular 'dog-days' weapons, and were subsequently lengthened to ease their use on horseback. At the same time the availability of metal promoted the use of other weapons, such as knife-clubs and the more common tomahawks. The very popular metal 'butcher knife' served as utilitarian tool, scalping-knife and weapon; and metal blades were used for spears and lances, in all cases replacing the laboriously crafted and fragile chipped stone heads. Lances were both weapons and symbols of office and bravery. The bow-lance, for example, was carried by Cheyenne Bowstring Society members, while many tribes used decorated staffs, often shaped like a shepherd's crook and covered in otter fur (and sometimes mistakenly called coup-sticks) to identify officers.

The shield completed the warrior's physical defences, and once again evolved with the use of the horse, being reduced from approximately 3 ft to between $1\frac{1}{2}$ and 2 ft diameter. While its construction of one or two layers of heavy buffalo hide, shrunk by heating and padded with hair or feathers, was capable of deflecting a low-velocity musket ball, much of the shield's protection was believed to lie in the 'medicine' of the designs and regalia it displayed. This decoration was believed to imbue the owner with supernatural defences, perhaps through depicting his vision-spirit—for example, by a painting of a bear claw, or the actual attachment of a real claw to the shield. A great deal of ritual surrounded the construction of a 'medicine-shield', and great care had to be taken in maintaining it. Taboos had to be observed: shields were prevented from touching the ground, and kept on tripods facing the sun to renew their power. The belief in the shield's spiritual power was such that sometimes only the thin protective cover, a miniature of the shield or a lacework shield were actually carried into battle.

Warrior Societies

Warrior societies were an important aspect of Plains life, dividing a tribe's fighting men into distinct units which provided their members with a social club, and an organisation in which they could progress through ranks of officership which brought great prestige. Each society had its own distinctive songs, dances and costume, and held regular meetings of its members. They also served the purposes of providing a policing force, encouraging bravery through inter-society rivalry, and providing a medium through which the civil chiefs and warriors could confer.

There were two distinct types of warrior society, 'graded' and 'non-graded'. The Blackfoot, Arapaho, Gros Ventre, Mandan, Hidatsa and Kiowa all used a graded system, conforming to the same general pattern. As a group of boys of a similar age became old enough to fight, they would offer a pipe and gifts to their immediate seniors, the members of the most junior society, in order to buy the right to their songs, dances, ceremonies and regalia, and consequent membership of the club. Once the sellers of membership had negotiated the maximum fee they would agree acceptance by smoking the pipe. They were then feasted by the young buyers, helped out by their relatives, while they taught them the appropriate rituals. This completed, the

This war shirt, collected in 1837, is possibly Crow. The upper part is stained with red ochre, and it is embellished with long fringes, quillwork and beadwork. (Berne Historical Museum)

new society members would proudly announce their new status. Those men who had sold them membership did not remain in the society, however; they were displaced, and subsequently sought to buy themselves into the next grade up. This process was repeated until a man sold his membership of the most senior society in the tribe, and retired as a recognised warrior.

Each society in the graded system was accorded a definite rank, so that there was no doubt as to which held greatest seniority. Since a warrior would only seek purchase into the next society when he had gained enough experience from his current fraternity, and promotion was sought by a body of men rather than an individual, the societies were approximately graded by age and achievement.

In contrast, the non-graded societies, typified by those of the Crow, Cheyenne, Sioux, Assiniboin, Pawnee and Arikara, were theoretically equivalent in status, although the popularity of each varied according to the exploits of its members. The societies did not generally discriminate between those wishing to join their ranks, since a substantial membership was important for the club's survival. Those warriors whom the society thought would improve their status were lured by gifts, while a man's relatives often affiliated themselves to his society. Occasionally a warrior would change societies either to replace a dead relative, or in the case of a disagreement. Because there was no formal grading of clubs inter-society rivalry was intense, with each vying for superiority. The Crow Lumpwood and Fox clubs took this to extremes, practising the formalised abduction of each other's members' wives. The fierce rivalry thus engendered was carried on to the battlefield, where each society strove to strike the first coup, and its members fought fearlessly out of duty towards their fraternity.

The duties of the graded and non-graded societies were very similar, and both were divided up into various honorary ranks. These offices were often two-sided, for while they conferred great honour, they also usually demanded some personal sacrifice or commitment. For instance, a 'bear-belt wearer' in the Big Dog Society of the Crow would pronounce his status by wearing a belt of bearskin complete with claws, by daubing his body with mud, and by rolling up his hair into tight balls imitating a bear's ears. While such an officer would receive privileges, such as eating first at a feast, acceptance of the rank would also entail the commitment to walk straight up to the enemy, regardless of safety; never to retreat; and to rescue any tribesman in danger.

Similar vows were common for both individuals and particular societies. Such warriors as the members of the Kiowa Koitsenko or Ten Bravest, and certain members of the Miwatani or Tall Ones of the Sioux and the renowned Cheyenne Dog Soldiers—all élite societies pledging unflinching bravery—would wear a sash which they staked to the ground in battle. There they would fight until victory or death, unless a fellow society member pulled up the stake and released them from their vow.

Perhaps the most extreme examples of recklessness were the 'contrary' warriors, who pledged themselves—out of grief, or foolhardiness, or in accordance with a vision of the much feared Thunder—to behave inversely, saying and doing everything opposite to the norm. Contrariness was a recurrent theme in Plains religion—the Blackfoot Sun Dancer, for instance, received cuts in his skin of the opposite depth to that which he had requested—and, similarly, the contrary warrior was believed to possess great power.

The Cheyenne had particular warrior societies for the contraries, such as the Bowstring Society; such men were formidable enemies, since, confident of their power and burdened by the restrictions of their rôle, they fought without fear. They would refrain from joining battle if victory was inevitable, charging in to fight ferociously only when their comrades were defeated. The Crow 'crazy dogs wishing to die' actively sought their own deaths.

Going to the opposite extreme, a man could opt out of the military scheme altogether, becoming a 'berdache' or transvestite. Such a decision stemmed from a vision in which a boy was offered the choice of a bow or pack strap by the Moon, and was handed the pack strap if he hesitated, thus symbolising his feminised future. Upon reaching manhood he would follow his nature and begin dressing, speaking and behaving as a woman. Like the contraries, berdaches both suffered ostracism and enjoyed power. Their effeminacy made them popular as matchmakers, and they were also sought-after to accompany war parties, both for their medical skills and because they were believed to bestow strength and virility upon the fighters. The berdaches also suffered scorn, however, since they represented the complete opposite of the 'fearless warrior' ideal.

War Costume

While a certain basic wardrobe was reserved simply for everyday comfort, the Plains warrior also wore highly decorative dress or war costume for ceremonies, parades, burial and battle, with embellishments which served various purposes. Firstly, display costume could denote society or

A buffalo skin robe of Mandan workmanship, pre-1837. It is decorated with a circular presentation of a war bonnet in black, surrounded by pictographs of deeds of war—possibly those of the Mandan chief Mato-tope. (Berne Historical Museum)

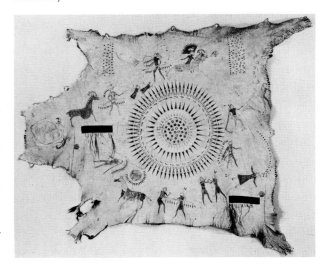

tribal rank, or membership of a visionary cult. Secondly, designs reflected visionary experience and consequently invoked 'medicine', providing supernatural guidance and protection. Thirdly, war costume displayed achievement marks, retaining and proclaiming evidence of a warrior's accomplishments.

The war shirt or 'scalp shirt' provides a good example of all three functions. In early years it was almost exclusively worn as a badge of office; this is most clearly illustrated by the leaders of the Sioux, who were called Shirt-Wearers, each being presented with a painted shirt fringed with hair symbolising the people they were responsible for. Prominent warriors, when they wore scalp-shirts as marks of distinction, fringed the neck and sleeves either with hair taken from an enemy or—particularly among the Blackfoot and Crow—with ermine pendants. Bands of beadwork or quillwork along the arms and over the shoulders, or in the form of rosettes, also denoted military excellence; among the Crow, for example, four such bands symbolised a holder of the four main coups.

War shirts were also decorated with painted representations of exploits, the symbols for different coups varying from tribe to tribe. Some commonly used designs were a hand, representing success in hand-to-hand combat; stripes, which could symbolise wounds or coups; pipes, numbering the war-parties led; and hoofmarks, indicating numbers of horses captured.

While a war shirt could therefore provide a pictographic record of the wearer's coups, it also offered him supernatural protection through other designs and trimmings. Such shirts, which might form a vital part of a man's war medicine, sometimes offered protection by association with the danger: for example, by depicting black dots or 'tadpoles' which supposedly made the wearer immune to bullets. Alternatively, shirts were painted with designs of a natural helper seen by the wearer in a vision, such as the bear or eagle, which could impart protection from the Sacred Powers. Pierced shirts were also worn as supernatural defences.

Shirts were not the only items of costume which were important for their decoration. Coups and medicine beliefs were also represented on robes, leggings and moccasins. The large surface area of

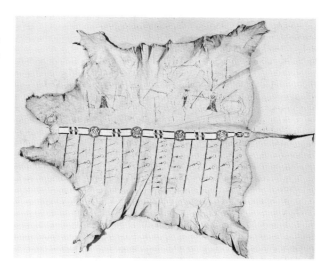

Buffalo robe, decorated from head to tail with a broad band and rosettes of quill- and beadwork. Above the band pairs of fighting men are painted in red and black; below it are 12 parallel lines with a series of symbols. (Berne Historical Museum)

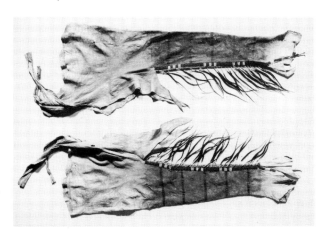

A Blackfoot man's leggings. The top half of each is stained with red ochre, the lower part dark brown with five horizontal brown stripes painted on. Beaded strips, predominantly turquoise blue with white stripes, are sewn down the length; and the fringing is of scalp locks of dark brown human hair.

robes was ideal for detailed pictographs; while leggings were fringed with hair in the same way as shirts, as well as painted with protective and honorific designs such as stripes. Moccasins were beaded with various intricate designs, and were also fringed; a Crow coup striker, for example, wore wolf tails at his heels.

Full costume was undoubtedly worn into battle, and not just reserved for ceremonial occasions. Warriors carried it until the enemy were sighted; then they would generally prepare for battle by donning their war costume, preparing any other regalia, applying face and body paint, and even

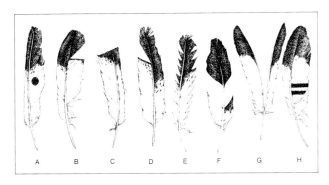

Examples of feather 'heraldry'. This varied considerably from tribe to tribe; besides various different ways of cutting or painting the feather, the type of feather and the position in which it was worn were also significant. **(A)** With red spot— 'killed an enemy'. **(B)** 'Killed an enemy and took his scalp'. **(C)** 'Cut an enemy's throat'. **(D)** 'Third coup'. **(E)** 'Fourth coup'. **(F)** 'Fifth coup'. **(G)** 'Has been wounded many times'. **(H)** Two red stripes—'third coup'.

rebraiding their hair. The reasons for such preparation were quite complex. Firstly, according to the Cheyenne warrior Wooden Leg, warriors dressed for death, just as they did when seriously ill. Secondly, the preparations for battle, performed with appropriate ceremony, put the warrior in touch with the sources of supernatural power, his regalia reminding him constantly of his spiritual obligations. Finally, a warrior's dress reflected his intentions and status, displaying his proven strength and courage, and asserting his confidence and superiority. Those warriors, therefore, who chose to fight virtually naked neither feared death nor needed physical protection, since they were convinced that their charms, paint and prayer fortified them against the enemies' weapons.

Naturally, the importance of costume extended to weapons and accessories. Again, coups were denoted, particularly by painting weapons; the Mandan chief Four Bears wore a red-painted knife in his hair and carried a lance of the same colour to symbolise that he had killed with those weapons. Status was signified by society lances and sashes, while medicine was also invoked, most obviously by the designs on shields but also by the use of special weapons, such as the Blackfoot knife set into a bear-claw hilt. Warriors also wore or carried objects which had a purely spiritual purpose. These 'war medicines' took various forms, from the popular leather pouch containing symbols of a warrior's power, to dolls, pendants, pipes, hoops and feathers. Such items were fixed to shields, worn around the neck or in the hair, carried, or possibly left in camp if

their nature was such that simple ownership conferred power. Reliance on them was great, whether they were an individual's personal talismans or those of the leader or 'pipe-holder' of a war-party. The warriors would smoke the leader's pipe and meditate upon his medicine to invoke its guidance, as well as following their own rituals, culminating in the ceremonial preparation for combat.

A warrior's apparel was usually completed by paint, and feathers worn in the hair. Systems of feather heraldry were employed by the Sioux and such tribes as the Hidatsa, Crow, Gros Ventre, Mandan and Assiniboin. Plumes from birds of prey, particularly the brown-tipped white feathers of the immature golden eagle, were cut, painted and positioned on the head (see diagram) to denote coups in the same way as the symbols used on costume. The specific meanings of different feather designs varied from tribe to tribe, and between individuals.

While any warrior could wear feathers, the right to wear an eagle feather war bonnet was earned only by a few. A warrior would first put on the bonnet either when he himself felt worthy of it or at the urgings of his superiors. To do so was a

Arapaho war bonnet, once owned by Yellow Calf. (British Museum)

First half of 19th century:
1: Hidatsa 'Dog-Soldier'
2, 3: Assiniboin warriors

A

Blackfoot:
1: Motokiks women's society member
2: Blood warrior
3: Warrior in winter dress
4: Elder

B

Blackfoot:
1: Mother with child
2: Grandmother
3, 4: Minipoka

C

D

Arapaho:
1: White Woman
2: Ghost Dancer, 1890

E

Kiowa and Comanche:
1: Kiowa brave
2: Kiowa woman
3: Comanche brave
4: Comanche girl

F

Little Bighorn, 25 June 1876:
1: Cheyenne brave
2: Buffalo Calf Road Woman
3: Crow scout

Blackfoot straight-up headdress—see Plate B4. (British Museum)

profession of his belief in his own fighting ability, and an assumption, therefore, of great responsibility. A bonnet-wearer claimed to be one of his tribe's ablest defenders, and as such he was expected to set an example of bravery, despite being an obvious target for enemy coup-seekers. The feathers in war bonnets were symbolic of coups among those tribes practising heraldry, and flags bearing further plumes also symbolised the carrier's bravery as well as providing a rallying point for fellow warriors.

Headdresses, sometimes centred on stuffed birds, were also worn as medicine items or to signify membership of a society, the members of the Miwatani Society wearing bonnets of eagle-owl feathers.

Face and body paint established the Indian in the rôle of a warrior. While certain colours could have specific meanings (black, for instance, often signifying victory), and while coup marks were used and old wounds highlighted, a warrior's war paint designs were usually only significant to him. Together with solemn prayers and vows, and the warrior's sacred costume and regalia, these designs completed the medicine preparations which fortified him for war.

Religion, Ceremony and Medicine

The Plains Indians believed that supernatural power pervaded every aspect of their life, and that to live in harmony with it was necessary to survival. This abstract force embraced all the natural mysteries of the Plains, so that not only their world but the very life the Indians led was considered sacred, and consequently their religion was a very real and practical belief.

A manifestation of spiritual power was called 'maxpé' by the Crow and 'wakan' by the Sioux, who therefore called a holy man a 'Wicasa-Wakan', and their supreme deity 'Wakan-Tanka' or the Great Spirit. 'Wakan' power was the source of what came to be known as medicine, so that 'making medicine' simply meant invoking the Sacred Powers. Medicine was sought and held through prayer, self-induced visions, ritual, and medicine items such as pipes and other bundles. It was so important because it provided for the tribe, and guided warriors and healers. The sacred right to invoke medicine had to be attained and preserved; and the life-sustaining force of the tribe, both in the abstract and in matters of material subsistence such as the buffalo, had to be renewed regularly.

The structure of the Indians' deities was complex, often loosely defined, and varied from tribe to tribe. A belief in a dominant force or supreme deity, the original source of medicine and controller of lesser spirits, was widespread. The lack of clarity that surrounded this being lay in the belief that it was both personified as a distinct Great Spirit, while also being seen as a part of everything, an omniscient force. The Cheyenne beliefs typify this, since while they recognised Ma'heo'o as the 'All-Father', their cosmology incorporated a group of subordinate deities emanating from the 'All-Father'. While these had distinct identities they could also be seen collectively as a single entity, 'Ma'heono', the Sacred Powers. Since medicine lay in all things, everything, including these Sacred Powers, was a part of the Great Spirit, whose power divided and sub-divided indefinitely.

The sun was generally the most powerful subsidiary power, the bringer of light and life. It was distinct from the Great Spirit, but they were closely integrated, since tribes commonly regarded the sun as a material token of the Great Spirit's existence. While the supreme deity was an abstract, the sun was a visible symbol, and the tipi was always pitched to face east so that prayers of thanks could be offered up to it at the beginning of each day.

The moon, sky and Earth were also venerated, as were the stars, the Morning and Evening Stars playing a large part in Pawnee ceremony. The Sacred Powers were commonly divided into two groups, the Cheyenne for instance recognising the Listeners-Above dominated by the sun, and the Listeners-Below dominated by the Earth. This idea of opposites, be they above and below, good and evil, male and female, was a consistent theme in the Plains religions; the Indians attempted to balance them, engendering power through harmony.

There were a number of other recurrent themes which reflected the constancy of religion. Tribal sites of great spiritual importance were common, usually isolated summits or places of natural wonder where medicine was most effectively sought through visions. To the Comanche, Medicine Bluff in the Wichita Mountains was important, while the Cheyenne called Bear Butte the Sacred Mountain, believing it to be the place where the All-Father met with their prophet Sweet Medicine, and the source of medicine on Earth.

The sacred circle, as the perfect form and the shape of natural phenomena such as the sun, was represented by the camp circle, the base of the tipi, and the performance of ceremonies in a clockwise, circular direction where possible, reflecting the movement of the sun. It was also divided by the sacred number four into the continuous life-pattern, at the semi-cardinal directions in the case of the Cheyenne. South-east represented renewal, south-west growth and nourishment, north-west maturity, and north-east completion of, and return along, the unbroken circle to renewal. This explains the importance of renewal in many ceremonies, as well as the emphasis placed on the number four. There were the Sacred Powers of the Four Winds and the Four Directions, and the number was also believed to permeate everything natural. Consequently, crosses were worn to symbolise the Four Directions, and the number figured significantly in ritual, ranging from four objects being used, to three feints being made before a movement was completed.

Oglala Sioux 'trailer' war bonnet from the Pine Ridge Reservation in South Dakota. (Berne Historical Museum)

The Vision Quest

The Indians believed that to distinguish themselves, and indeed to survive, they needed to acquire medicine from the Sacred Powers through visionary experience. Dreams came to the fortunate involuntarily when they were children, and as they grew up further knowledge revealed the full extent of their blessing. Most, however, had to reach out for power, invoking the aid of the Great Spirit through self-sacrifice. Usually, as a boy approached manhood, he would seek out a shaman to instruct and assist him in his 'vision quest', and together they decided the time and method of the youngster's undertaking.

To begin with, the vision-seeker would usually purify himself in a 'sweat lodge', a low dome of willow saplings covered with skins to retain the scorching vapours given off by water poured on to red-hot rocks placed in a central pit. Sage was also burnt or rubbed on the body, and paint applied in sacred designs.

The vision quest itself was endured in a place of solitude, allowing the vision-seeker to concentrate fully upon the Sacred Powers. The actual form it took varied, but it usually involved the vision-seeker remaining alone in the same spot for an agreed number of days and nights, perhaps broken up by visits from his supervising shaman. Some would sit in the darkness of a small lodge, some would remain unsheltered, while others stood in one spot staring at the sun to force themselves to stay awake. Sioux vision-seekers paced out a cross from a central pole to poles marking the Four Directions, hung with offerings of tobacco and red flannel strips.

The vision-seeker was naked apart from perhaps a breechclout and moccasins, and shunned all earthly protection other than a buffalo robe for warmth at night. Sacred objects such as a buffalo skull, sage, and buffalo chips were used to forge a link with the Sacred Powers, as was a pipe, which carried the prayers of the vision-seeker to the Great Spirit. Food and drink were abstained from for the duration of the quest, so that, with his mind resting inexorably on the Great Spirit, the vision-seeker, weak from hunger and thirst, might achieve a vision. Some attempted to accelerate the effect through self-sacrifice, chopping off a finger joint, for instance, offering up their very flesh to the Great Spirit, as well as weakening themselves through loss of blood and so encouraging a trance.

Those who failed to see a portent of their medicine either resigned themselves to failure or prolonged their ordeal. Weak and alone, the successful vision-seekers would either see or hear a sign of their medicine while conscious, or, semi-conscious, they would drift from fitful sleep into a trance revealing a vivid apparition. Some fainted

Little Wolf, Sweet Medicine Chief of the Cheyenne; and, seated, Morning Star (Dull Knife), Chief of the Northern Cheyenne, photographed during a delegation to Washington in 1873. (Smithsonian Institution, courtesy Robin May)

from lack of food, drink, sleep, or blood, and discovered spiritual help when close to death.

The actual visions which men saw were obviously very varied, but as the power of the Great Spirit was believed to be diffused throughout the Indians' natural surroundings, it was in a comprehensible, natural form that medicine was most often revealed, the commonest visions being of birds and animals. Birds could impart the powers which were characteristic of their own abilities, from the arrogant, ferocious skills of the eagle, through the agility of the kingfisher, to the knowledge and acute hearing of the tiny chickadee. Animals provided medicine in the same way, the buffalo, for example, signifying hunting success or abundant food, or imparting its powers of strength and tenacity.

Birds and animals, as well as being able to impart abilities to the dreamer in their own right, might also be seen as messengers from the Sacred Powers, the owl, for example, sometimes being seen as a servant of the moon.

Thus a vivid dream of an encounter with, or even the distant sound of, a bird or animal might fulfil the vision-seeker's quest, assuring him of a natural medium through which to attain his medicine by providing him with a personal supernatural guardian or 'vision spirit'. Alternatively, the vision-seeker might see himself, displaying his medicine by his actions. He could be wearing special clothing or paint and riding a horse bearing painted symbols, while displaying invulnerability by riding through a hail of bullets, arrows, or even lightning bolts. An animal guardian might also be revealed through some adornment, such as a bear claw necklace; or by a natural power, such as the eagle, saving him from danger.

A vision had to be interpreted before it could be fully understood, so the visionary would receive instruction from his tribe's shamans, or possibly from a 'dream cult'. These comprised a small membership who had all seen the same vision spirit, and could share and represent their medicine collectively, while enhancing their prestige. Each cult developed specific ceremony and regalia derived from the appearance and actions of their supernatural patron; thus Bear Cult members mimicked the bear, invoking medicine known to provide guidance in both war and doctoring.

The relationship between a visionary and his vision spirit can be seen in the sense of an adoption. The vision spirit would direct its spiritual son in the use of its imbued power, outlining the necessary ritual, paint, song, dress and taboos. An intrinsic idea underlying this was that medicine was a tangible substance which was transferable, from the Sacred Powers to nature, from nature to the

Indians, and subsequently from one man to another. The vision spirit was regarded as having offered a part of itself to the visionary, a share in its personal medicine. The rest of the visionary's life was then spent under a spiritual protection and obligation, fulfilling the requirements of his vision.

Initially, he secured his relationship with the Sacred Powers by forming his acquired medicine into a palpable object, called a 'medicine bundle'. This could take many forms, from an actual bundle of talismans to charms centred around a pipe; even a medicine shield was a form of 'bundle'. Derivatives from this included necklaces, clothing, feathers, adornments hung from shields, small medicine pouches and even the paint a man wore, all of which, along with appropriate ritual, invoked and retained a man's medicine. Often they worked through association, so that medicine acquired from the eagle might be represented by an eagle skin bundle containing charms outlined in the vision, an eagle feather worn in the hair, a single talon pendant hung around the neck, and a complete claw attached to a painted shield.

Subsequent meditation and ritual provided receptive visionaries with medicines from different sources; for instance, Weasel Tail of the Blood Blackfoot possessed a wide variety of medicines, regarding the otter, king-bird, and weasel all as personal helpers, and consequently owning a complex range of bundles. Provision was also made, however, for those men who failed to achieve a vision. Since medicine was transferable, they were able to purchase a share of power from a more fortunate visionary, who would assume the paternal rôle in the standard adoption.

Certain men and women received visions of particular spiritual significance, which portended a future as a shaman. Such visions were usually distinguishable by the fact that rather than simply offering power, they also conferred a degree of understanding. This ranged from the visionary being taught the use of certain herbs in healing, to his being made aware of the sacred nature of the world. The Sioux Black Elk was shown by the Sacred Powers that 'the sacred hoop of my people was one of many hoops that made one circle'; and in such a way was given a comprehension of spiritual matters.

The main distinction made between shamans

(A) Sioux tomahawk pipe (B) Crow medicine pipe (C) Northern Plains pipe dating from after 1850 (D) Crow sacred pipe, c.1850

was that between priests and doctors. Doctors were those shamans who used their supernatural power, possibly together with herbal remedies and rites learnt from their elders, to heal. A priest was a spiritual advisor and interpreter. Taught through study under an experienced holy man, and sanctioned by visionary experience, he was responsible for the preservation of tribal lore, relics and ceremony, and for the direction of spiritual affairs.

One important rôle played by the priests was that of ritual keepers of the tribal bundles. These were medicines of tribal, rather than individual significance, exemplified by the huge Beaver Bundle of the Blackfoot. This was the largest of all tribal bundles, symbolising nearly all birds and animals through the numerous skins it contained, as well as being the 'father' of the other Blackfoot bundles, since it also held aspects of each of them. It originated from the Beaver, who taught the first keeper the sacred songs which accompanied the bundle's ceremonies; and since it was very sacred, the keeper's rôle was equally revered. His spiritual obligations were to memorise the ceremonies and songs (originally over 400 of them) to conduct the rituals and maintain the bundle, to possess the knowledge of the associated medicines, and to live a life in harmony with nature. The Beaver Bundle was opened to offer a general blessing, as part of tribal ceremonies of renewal and to overcome illness and hunger. The keeper also used its potent medicine to predict the

The integrity of the US Government's reservation agents varied sharply. Some were well-meaning men doing their best under difficult circumstances; others were out-and-out swindlers, who did not care whether their Indians lived or died so long as their own opportunities for corruption were undisturbed. This photo shows an Indian agent with Arapaho braves.

weather and guide camp moves, and kept a calendar and recorded the 'winter counts' which formed the tribal history.

Tribal bundles, like all medicines, could be transferred. This was usually done formally, the keeper's neophyte inheriting the bundle and its obligations following years of study, thus ensuring its continued blessing upon the tribe. The old-time transfer of the Sacred Arrows of the Cheyenne entailed the new keeper—as a sign of his dedication to the Great Spirit or All-Father, and in appeal for His blessing—offering up numerous slices of his own flesh cut in sacred patterns, the scars of which remained for life.

The Sun Dance

Since their religion was such a constant practice, continuous acknowledgement of the Sacred Powers being important to maintain harmony, various simple forms of worship permeated the Indians' everyday lives.

Prayers and offerings were constantly offered up to the Sacred Powers. At their simplest they involved thanksgiving to the sun and the Great Spirit, or the offering of a morsel of food to the Sky and Earth; but they also extended to pledging a

Shun-ka Blo-ka or 'He-Dog' of the Oglala Sioux. It is said that when Crazy Horse and his followers surrendered at Camp Robinson on 6 May 1877, He-Dog placed his scalp shirt on Lt. W. P. Clarke to signify that war between them was at an end. (Smithsonian Institution, courtesy Robin May)

sacrifice of possessions, participation in a ceremony, or sacrifice of a man's flesh in exchange for safety or success in war or recovery from illness.

The smoke from a pipe carried prayers to the Sky, Mother Earth and the Four Directions, while the sacred number, circle and sunwise direction all provided a constant means of demonstrating awareness of spiritual obligations. The rituals that surrounded sacred objects were consistent with this. The ceremony that surrounded the opening of a medicine bundle, for instance, or the taboos that accompanied the use of medicine items, ensured careful observance of their sanctity.

The culmination of these rituals were the tribal ceremonies, the most important of which was the Sun Dance. This was a major tribal ceremony of all of the typical Plains tribes, apart from the Comanche, until 1874. It was held when the whole tribe was camped together—sometimes annually, as among the Blackfoot, and sometimes sporadically, as with the Crow. Since tribes formed the Sun Dance into a composite of their other ceremonies there were obviously tribal variations, but as it had been diffused from tribe to tribe there were also common features.

Primarily, the ceremony allowed the tribe as a whole to supplicate the Sacred Powers, while different tribes also had other distinct motives. To the Crow, it was a means of securing a vision promising revenge; to the Cheyenne, a ceremony of renewal. Underlying these tribal motives was the contractual vow taken by the central 'pledger' to sponsor the ceremony in exchange for divine favour, be it a safe return from war or recovery from illness. Similar vows, either taken for themselves or for relatives, also bound individuals to more minor rôles. Women always either assumed the rôle of central pledger—illustrated by the Sun Dance of the Blackfoot, which centred on a woman's purchase of the valuable Nataos Bundle and sponsorship of the ceremony—or at least played an important part.

The sacred number four was recurrent, this number of days often being set aside both for the preparatory ceremonies—illustrated by the 'Lone Tipi' rites of the Cheyenne—and for the main rituals of the Sun Dance. These were initially focused on the construction of the medicine lodge, a large building which housed the concluding ceremonies, situated in the middle of the camp circle and centred on a significant central pole.

The finding of a forked cottonwood tree suitable for this task involved a great deal of ritual, since the tree was treated as being symbolic of an enemy. Consequently, a privileged scout would usually be sent out to find it; and following his return to report the successful discovery of an enemy, the cottonwood was ceremonially 'killed' and coup counted on it. Some tribes, such as the Crow, reserved the right to notch the tree, before it was felled, for a virtuous woman.

When the central pole had been carried back to camp it was raised at the centre of the lodge. For the Blackfoot this completed the central pledger's rôle as she ended her fast, the cottonwood proclaiming her virtue if it was raised perfectly upright. The central pole remained steeped in symbolism, particularly the bushy fork at its top, which was seen by some tribes as the nest of the Thunderbird, and was commonly hung with offerings, for instance of tobacco or cloth. The pole was also usually hung

A Sioux warrior. Note the broad beaded strip on the blanket worn wrapped around the waist, and the breast plate of bone 'hair-pipes'.

the Buffalo Dance, the ritual killing of one or two buffalo, and the very important preparation and solemn consumption of the sacred buffalo tongues.

The most spectacular element of the Sun Dance was the self-torture of dancers who had pledged to offer their flesh in supplication of the Sacred Powers. While some men—such as the Blackfoot Weather Dancers, the Crow central pledger, and the Sioux first grade dancers—performed an arduous dance, bobbing up and down on their toes, blowing on an eagle-bone whistle, and staring at the Sun or central pole, others had the flesh of their breasts and backs pierced through by skewers.

Some attached these to buffalo skulls, which they dragged until the skewers broke free or they had walked a certain distance. Others were attached to poles and fell back on the skewers, which tore their flesh; while some, such as the highest grade of Sioux dancers, were actually suspended from the central pole by ropes to the skewers through their breasts, until the skewers broke free. The loose skin was cut off and placed at the central pole as a sacrifice to the sun.

Clearly, such participants in the Sun Dance made very receptive visionaries. (Their attendants sometimes unwittingly planted the skewers so deeply that the dancers could only tear them free if others jumped on them to add their weight.) The achievement of a vision by the central pledger was a necessary condition for the ending of the Crow Sun Dance. The self-torture dancers offered the ultimate sacrifice to the Sacred Powers, and demonstrated unquestioning faith in their religion, while completing the ceremonies, which served to unite the tribe in worship, and to renew their dedication for the year ahead.

Conquest

The 1851 Laramie Treaty attempted to resolve the fundamental problem of the increasing number of troops, traders, settlers, prospectors and other emigrants who were crossing and consequently destroying the ancestral homelands of the Plains nations. By offering material compensation to tribes in exchange for their acceptance of previously inconceivable boundaries and the establishment of roads and forts, the treaty provided an obviously

with effigies of some form. The Sioux painted it at the Four Directions, and hung up rawhide figures of the Whirlwind and Crazy Buffalo, two evil spirits who were later shot down by the tribe's warriors. The Crow and the Kiowa focused their ceremonies on a doll fixed to the central pole, the Kiowa using their sacred Tai-me doll, while an effigy was also contained in the Blackfoot Nataos Bundle head-dress.

A great number of ceremonies, usually preceded by fasting and purification rites by the important participants, were held around the central pole. There was dancing by both the men's and women's societies, as well as the recounting of coups by the tribe's warriors. An altar was always prominent, playing a central rôle in the Cheyenne ceremony as its construction symbolised the renewal of the Earth, and was commonly adorned with the painted skull of a buffalo. This sacred animal was also represented by such aspects of the Sun Dance as temporary solution. It was one in a series of agreements which failed or were broken, usually by the whites. In this case matters came to a head when US Army Lt. Grattan and his 30-man party were killed while impetuously and illegally attempting to arrest a Sioux warrior.

Years of alternating conflict and truce followed, resulting from a fundamental clash of cultures. The expanding, materialist society of the whites claimed land that was considered sacred by a spiritual people, and attempted to confine the essentially nomadic Plains Indians to ever-smaller territories. The defiant defeat of Gen. Custer at the Little Bighorn in 1876, by a force comprising mainly Sioux and Cheyennes, only served to provoke an increasingly ruthless campaign by the US Army.

One reason for the futility of the Indian cause was that they were divided by tribal feuds; Custer, for example, was guided to the Little Bighorn by Crow and Arikara scouts. A united Indian nation could have defended their lands more ably, but, in the words of Sitting Bull, they were 'an island of Indians in a lake of whites'.

This proud leader of the Hunkpapa Sioux had offered his blood to the Great Spirit by scarifying his arms, and performed the gazing-at-the-sun dance, to augur Custer's defeat, while at the same time prophesying that desire for the whites' goods would 'prove a curse to this nation'.

His warning was perceptive, for it was not only through war that the Plains Indians were defeated. Trade goods had established a certain Indian dependence on the whites, while also exposing them to the sad effects of alcohol, against which they had an unusually low tolerance. Foreign diseases such as smallpox, against which the Indians had no natural defences, wiped out whole bands at a time; while the destructive nature of the whites also took its toll through the callous slaughter of the buffalo herds. Following the Indians' considerably increased hunting efforts to meet trade demands, white professional hunters arrived by the 1860s. They left most of the meat from their kills rotting on the Plains, while securing so many hides that they disturbed migration patterns as well as reducing the buffaloes' overall numbers drastically. Some Army officers were well aware that by destroying their staff of life they were destroying the Plains Indians.

The most superficial comparison of white and Indian cultures shows us that the destruction of the latter was inevitable. Apart from the sheer numbers involved, and the whites' technological advantages; apart from the growing Indian dependence on white goods, and the parallel destruction of the buffalo herds which were the material basis of their lifestyle; apart from all these weaknesses, the Indians also suffered fatally when their attitude to warfare was confronted by the European military tradition of the whites.

The red man was the individual warrior supreme, and his courage, endurance, horsemanship and fieldcraft brought him many victories over the whites: but almost always on a strictly limited, local scale. It was almost unknown for the Indians to assemble an 'army' large enough to threaten seriously a major US column in pitched battle—thus the extraordinary trauma caused by the Custer massacre. It was terribly difficult for the Indians to hold such a force together in the field for more than a few weeks. The Plains warrior was, as we have seen, a hunter and provider too—war was only one facet of his life. The white trooper might be individually less impressive as a fighting man; but his dogged, plodding columns did not dwindle and drift apart as the riders became bored, tired, disheartened, or worried about their families. The trooper was the tool—in theory, and usually in practice—of a single overall command with a unified plan of campaign. The Indians, as we have seen, were always weakened by a disunity which must seem chronic to white eyes. But this is to misjudge the Indians—to apply to them, with hindsight, the military thought-patterns of an alien culture. Their disunity was not frivolous, but a natural aspect of the way of life which had formed them over the centuries.

By 1881 the last Indian bands were confined to reservations, which continued to diminish in size with every treaty signed and every treaty broken. The Indians fought back briefly through their religion, most notably through the 'Ghost Dance'. This was conceived in 1889 by a Paiute shaman named Wovoka, during a fever, and spread rapidly through the Plains tribes. It promised the appearance of a Messiah, together with the return of the buffalo and the Indian dead, to herald an Indian resurgence. Wovoka advocated peaceful, innocent behaviour as opposed to an armed uprising. Adherents to the new faith, men and women, also performed the Ghost Dance itself; the main ritual was a circular, shuffling dance, the participants increasing their speed as they sang until they fell into a trance, attaining visions of lost relatives and of the return of past splendour. Visions also revealed sacred designs which were used to embellish Ghost Dance shirts—which in the case of the Sioux tainted the original peaceful faith since they were provocatively proclaimed to make the wearer impervious to bullets.

The glimmer of hope that the Ghost Dance offered was consequently extinguished in late December 1890 when the white authorities, increasingly nervous at the prophecies of the religion, the warlike nature of protective shirts, and the frenzied support the cult had aroused, sent troops to intercept Big Foot's Miniconjou Sioux band who were travelling to collect rations. The band were taken to and surrounded at Wounded Knee Creek; and there, after the start of a Ghost Dance and the firing of a concealed gun by an Indian, Big Foot and a large number of his band were massacred, including many women and children. Conflicting figures have been given by various respected writers, ranging from 128 Indian dead to as many as several hundred, and thus reflecting the problems of accurately chronicling the Plains Indians. Records show that the known dead totalled 153, but to this can be added a number who died subsequently out of the authorities' care, possibly raising the true figure to nearer 180.

The Wounded Knee massacre symbolised the final destruction of the Plains Indians, through the breaking of their spirit.

The Plates

The exact dating of many of these costumes is impossible. Apart from certain general trends, such as the increased use of trade cloth in place of skins as the 19th century progressed, the same costumes were used over a long period.

A: Warriors of 1800–1850

Pictorial information as to the appearance of the Plains Indians before the invention of photography

The Cheyenne sub-chief Yellow Bear, a magnificent example of Cheyenne facial features. (Robin May collection)

is relatively scarce. What knowledge we have is due to artists such as Bodmer and Catlin, who took on the task of portraying the American Indian during the 1830s. We have relied heavily upon their work in illustrating this earlier period, supported by written descriptions and such few artefacts as survive. It is obvious that the garments were far less tailored than they subsequently became, being made of nearly complete skins of deer and sheep.

A1: Hidatsa 'Dog-Soldier' (warrior society member)

Under attack by two Assiniboin warriors, this Hidatsa has staked his long sash-end to the ground, symbolising his vow not to retreat before the enemy unless released by a fellow warrior. He also wears an elaborate feathered headdress, painted and quilled leggings, and quilled moccasins from which hang animal tails. A scalp hangs from his Missouri war hatchet, and he is also armed with a bow and arrows.

A2: Assiniboin warrior

His bow-lance, later to become a ceremonial object, is here used in earnest as a weapon. From his shoulders hangs a buffalo robe. He carries a painted shield complete with attached medicine bundle. It is worth noting that at this period shields were larger than they subsequently became with the development of horseback fighting.

Two Moon(s), a famous Northern Cheyenne warrior; born in 1842 or 1847, he lived until 1917, and is here photographed in a magnificent 'trailer' war bonnet at Ft Keogh in 1878. One of nine Northern Kit Fox 'little chiefs', Two Moon played a prominent part at the Little Bighorn in 1876. In 1913, while visiting Washington, he claimed to have led all the Cheyenne who fought at the Greasy Grass, but Black Wolf dismissed him as 'the biggest liar in the whole Cheyenne tribe'. To this Two Moon retorted that he did not think it wrong to lie to white people! After leading the last band of Cheyenne into Ft Keogh in April 1877, Two Moon became an influential figure; he scouted against the Nez Percé and the Sioux under Col. Nelson 'Bear Coat' Miles, and the whites regarded him as the Chief of the Northern Cheyenne. In fact his own people continued to recognise their own band chiefs, not acknowledging Two Moon as an 'old man chief' until his later years. (National Park Service, US Dept. of the Interior, courtesy Robin May)

A3: Assiniboin warrior
Armed with a typical 'gun-stock' club, he wears a headdress of small feathers and horns, and a typical war shirt and leggings of this early period, decorated with quillwork and paint.

B: The Blackfoot
B1: Member of the Motokiks women's society
In traditional costume, it is impossible to date this figure closely; early skin garments were retained for these purposes after trade cloth had begun to predominate in everyday clothing. Society membership is marked by the so-called 'scabby bull' headdress. The skin dress is decorated with elk teeth, and held at the waist by a long 'tack' belt—i.e. a leather belt decorated with brass tacks. Beaded leggings and moccasins complete the costume. She holds a pipe bag.

B2: Blood warrior
This member of the Blood sub-group of the tribe decorates his hair with strips of ermine. His war medicine hangs from his left shoulder: a bandolier of large seeds, and a bunch of owl and hawk feathers. He wears a cloth shirt with beaded strips—both indicating a mid-19th century date, perhaps—a breechclout, and moccasins. He carries an English-made flintlock musket decorated by him with brass tacks, as is the whip/war club hanging from his right wrist. A 'strike-a-light' (flint-and-steel) hangs from his gun. His shield is hung on his left hip. The end of the long tack belt hangs almost to the ground.

B3: Warrior in winter dress, second half of the 19th century
His fur hat is decorated with a solitary eagle feather. The capote or hooded blanket coat, introduced originally by French trappers in the north-east, is made from a striped Hudson's Bay trade blanket. On a leather shoulder strap hang a horn container of some kind—not a powder horn, since he carries a breech-loader—and a spyglass in a leather case. He carries his rifle in a beaded gun case, and a beaded knife sheath is attached to his tack belt. The leggings are also of blanket cloth.

B4: Elder
The ornate bonnet is of the type known as a 'straight up' headdress; it is made of eagle feathers decorated with strips of quillwork, tipped with ermine and horse hair; a cap of ermine, and ermine pendants; and a brow band decorated with brass tacks. The weasel tail shirt—so-called for obvious reasons—is decorated with beaded strip, and over it hangs a bead-wrapped loop necklace. Wrapped around his body and over his left shoulder he wears a blanket decorated with a beaded blanket strip hung with ermine pendants. Floral beaded moccasins complete the costume. In his right hand he carries a pipe and a pipe bag decorated with quill- and beadwork; in his left, a horse stick—an item of war medicine consisting of a carved stick with a horse's head, leather ears, a scalp of black horse hair, coloured buffalo wool and horse tail, adorned with two arrows with leather heads.

C: Three generations of the Blackfoot
C1: Blackfoot mother with child in cradleboard
She wears an old-style buckskin dress decorated with beads and elk teeth. A broad leather tack belt can just be seen at the waist. The cradleboard, traditionally made from curved and cross-braced willow wands, was later replaced by a board sawn to this shape. It is covered with buckskin decorated with floral beadwork, as is the apron which covers the lacing holding the baby. The carrying strap passes round the mother's shoulders and chest; it also allowed the cradleboard to be hung from a saddle pommel or a convenient tree.

C2: Grandmother
She wears a trade cloth headscarf, a sateen trade cloth dress decorated with beads and cowrie shells, shell earrings and many necklaces. She smokes a woman's pipe, and at her feet are her smoking accessories: a cutting board, twist of tobacco, knife, tamping sticks, and a steel for fire-making (also used for sharpening knives).

C3: Minipoka
Loosely translated, a 'favourite', recognisable by the exact replica of an adult female costume which has been lovingly made for her. The blanket dress is decorated with cowrie shells and ribbon; her leggings and moccasins are decorated with bead-work. The doll that she carries is another near-perfect replica of adult costume, down to the detail of a 'strike-a-light' hanging from its belt.

C4: Minipoka
Another lovingly-detailed costume for a special child. He has a split-horn bonnet decorated with weasel strips, ribbons, bells and eagle feathers; a beaded and painted skin shirt; a breechclout, blanket leggings and moccasins, all decorated with typical Blackfoot beadwork. In his left hand is a doll; in his right, a hoop-and-stick game, designed to develop marksmanship—the idea was to throw the feathered stick through the rolling hoop.

D: Fight between Sioux and Crow warriors, mid- to late 19th century
D1: Sioux, Tokala or Kit Fox Society
The society costume consisted of a fox pelt and tail, worn here as a headdress although it could also be

Wolf Robe, a Southern Cheyenne born c.1841, and here photographed in 1909. (Smithsonian Institution, courtesy Robin May)

worn as a sash or belt. Another symbol was the unstrung bow-lance, decorated with beadwork and hung with a loose-flowing cluster of feathers ending in two eagle feathers. He also carries a painted shield and a beaded bowcase and quiver.

On his chest is a 'hair-pipe' breast plate. In the earliest days these thin tubes were made from the central column of the conch shell. By the 17th century white traders were already supplying brass replicas, and silver examples appeared in the 18th century. These metal tubes were unpopular, and before the end of the century traders were supplying shell tubes from New Jersey. Used individually as hair ornaments (thus 'hair-pipes'), they reached the Plains early in the 1800s, and spread as far as the Cheyenne. They were also grouped in large numbers as necklaces, and finally as breast plates. White-manufactured bone hair-pipes were popular for breast plates in the second half of the century.

A breechclout, old-style beaded skin leggings and beaded moccasins complete his costume. His horse blanket is decorated with both quillwork and beadwork.

D2: Sioux, Cante Tinza or Braveheart Society
The society is recognised by the headdress, the feathered lance, and the sabre (captured or traded) with a hanging black otter skin, which was carried by some officers of the society. The headdress is made from split buffalo horns, with ermine

43

American Horse, a 'Shirt-Wearer' of the Oglala Sioux; the photograph has been captioned elsewhere as having been taken during a delegation to Washington in 1877, but American Horse was already dead by that date. He was fatally wounded in the stomach on 9 September 1876 by soldiers from Gen. George Crook's command, who destroyed his winter camp and appropriated dried buffalo meat for much-needed rations. Note his finely beaded scalp shirt. (Smithsonian Institution, courtesy Robin May)

decorations, a beaded brow band, and a cloth trailer with four lines of eagle feathers. The beaded war shirt is decorated with paint, and horse and human hair. Beaded moccasins are worn with blanket leggings.

D3: Sioux, Kangi Yuha or Crow Owner Society
The marks of the society are the stuffed crow hung round his neck, the black body paint, and the decorations of feathers, otter skin wrap and stuffed crow upon his lance. Another identifying sign is the fact that the undersides of the war shirt sleeves have not been sewn but are only thonged together, allowing him to throw them back for greater freedom of movement in combat. His painted shield hangs from his horse. He is armed with a Colt single-action .45 revolver.

D4: Sioux, Miwatani Society
Also known as the Tall Ones and the Owl Feather Headdress Order, this society wore headdresses of owl feathers surrounding four upright eagle feathers; whistles made from eagle wing bones; and quirts with straps and trailers of otter skin. They, too, wore a 'stake-down' sash. In his right hand is a coup stick, in his left a bow; the society fletched its arrows with owl feathers. He also wears a breechclout and beaded moccasins.

D5: Sioux, Wiciska or White Marked Society
The headdress consists of split horns and an eagle feather trailer; another mark of membership is the hooked lance. In his left hand he carries a club. He wears a bird claw necklace, a quilled breast plate, a quilled knife case, and beaded moccasins, and the painted shield is embellished with bells and feathers.

D6: Crow warrior
Armed with a typical lance, he wears an eagle skin on his head; a shirt decorated with typical Crow beadwork and ermine; quilled and painted leggings, and quilled moccasins. His painted shield is heavily decorated with feathers hung from a lower apron.

D7: Crow warrior
The magnificent headdress of a bear's head and skin and eagle feathers is worn with typical Crow necklaces, a trade cloth breechclout, old-style beaded leggings, and moccasins. The painted shield is decorated with feathers, and the Winchester carbine with brass tacks.
(This plate is based upon the pictographs of Amos Bad Heart Bull, an Oglala Sioux from the Pine Ridge Reservation.)

E: The Arapaho
E1: White Woman
The White Woman was the key figure in the ceremonies of the Arapaho women's Buffalo Society in the earlier part of the 19th century. Her regalia consists of a headdress of swan and goose feathers and down, white weasel skins and buffalo horns; and a wide belt beaded with crosses and bars, hung with buffalo tails, white feathers, and the skins of whip-poor-will and poor-will birds. Her ceremonial dress is decorated with painted symbols and beadwork, and her leggings and moccasins are typical of the fine craftsmanship of the Arapaho.

She holds a whistle in her mouth, and carries two wooden poles which were used to imitate the pounding of buffalo hooves during the ceremony.

E2: Ghost Dancer, 1890
In contrast to the figure of White Woman, representing the early Plains rituals, this illustration shows a participant in the Ghost Dance—the religion of desperation which spread from the Paiutes of Nevada right across the Plains in 1889–90. He is presenting a ceremonial pipe to the Sun, Earth, Fire, and Four Winds prior to passing it to the other dancers. He wears as little as possible to connect him with the white man—e.g. metal. Many Ghost Dancers went so far as to avoid beadwork (since trade beads had a white connotation) or even cloth; but due to the times he lives in this dancer is forced to wear a cloth breechclout, and retains his moccasins. The painted symbols on his Ghost Dance shirt and leggings have a ceremonial significance.

F: The Kiowa and Comanche
Leaving the Rocky Mountains area and travelling south at some time during the early 18th century, these tribes eventually reached the southern Plains. Both were renowned for their adventurous spirit, and the Comanche, in particular, for their horsemanship.

F1: Kiowa brave
Resplendent in a decorated fur turban, he wears a typical southern Plains hide shirt, far more tailored than those favoured by more northerly tribes. His braids are wrapped in elaborate otter skin drops. On his chest is a bone hair-pipe breast plate, from which hangs a pectoral of German silver. Across his lap are his bow case and quiver of mountain lion skin and beadwork. The decorative tabs of his leggings can be seen hanging from beneath the blanket wrapped round his waist. Behind him is his shield, complete with a large bell. In his left hand he carries a medicine arrow-lance, more a ceremonial object than a serious weapon.

F2: Kiowa woman
It is worth comparing the style of her dress with those of the more northerly tribes on earlier plates. The dress has an elaborately cut yoke, but little

Red Cloud, 1822–1909—the renowned leader of the Oglala Sioux, who proved as effective an enemy of the white man through diplomacy as through war. In the mid-1860s he advised the US Army: 'If you want peace, return at once to the Powder River'. When the warning was ignored he completely disrupted the Bozeman Trail from 1866 to 1868; commanded the famous massacre of Capt. Fetterman's 80 men; and forced the whites to reach a settlement on his terms. It was only after the troops had been withdrawn and the forts burned down that Red Cloud added his signature to the Treaty of Ft. Laramie, and retired from the warpath to a spacious reservation. Although he was criticised by the Sioux who remained hostile, he continued to be the most powerful Oglala chief. He obstructed the whites through intelligent diplomacy, securing agencies on the White River in 1873, making military supervision impractical, and, in 1875, demanding an impossible $600 million for the sale of the revered Black Hills of Dakota.

beadwork. It is made from three deerskins, one each for the front and back of the skirt and the third for the bodice. At the waist is a belt decorated with large German silver discs, from which hangs a beautifully beaded flint-and-steel pouch. The typical Kiowa leg-moccasins are decorated with metal bosses and delicate beadwork. Her child peeps out from the safety of a superbly decorated cradle.

F3: Comanche brave
Many Plains Indians were photographed wearing

various headgear obtained from the whites. This is an old 'Jeff Davis' or 'Hardee' military hat, last used in any numbers by the US Army just before the Civil War, during which it was seen in quantity only in Gen. Gibbons' famous 'Iron Brigade' from Wisconsin, Indiana and Michigan. Beneath his blanket this Comanche wears another southern Plains shirt, fringed and decorated with feathers. His hair dressing, chest ornament, long breechclout, heavily fringed leggings and moccasins are all typical of Comanche costume. He carries a fan of feathers and beadwork, and a spontoon-bladed tomahawk.

F4: Comanche girl

Again, the very limited use of beadwork is typical of the southern Plains tribes. The simplicity of her dress is made up for by the beauty and complexity of her boots of leather and rawhide, decorated with beads and German silver buttons, and painted green with a pigment extracted from pond algae.

G: Battle of the Little Bighorn, 25 June 1876
G1: Cheyenne brave

The Troops of the 7th Cavalry wiped out with Custer were C, E, F, I and L; their guidons were lost, though one was recovered 11 weeks later at Slim Buttes. This brave has seized the guidon of Troop L (identified by the letter in the centre of the ring of stars), and is about to use it as a more than adequate coup stick.

His war bonnet, quirt, saddle blanket, knife case and moccasins are based upon examples in the Haffenreffer Museum of Anthropology. Moccasins, knife case, saddle blanket, and the brow band of the bonnet are all good examples of typical mid-century Cheyenne beadwork: 'lazy stitch' on rawhide. The quirt is attached to his right wrist in the same way as that of G3; its heavy handle makes it a useful club.

According to Cheyenne sources, 12 warriors who fought at the Little Bighorn ('Greasy Grass') wore war bonnets, and ten of these were the type with trailers. As explained in the body of our text, the bonnet did not necessarily denote a chief, as is often supposed; but that the warrior had earned, and claimed, the right and honour of wearing it as a leading brave. The costume is completed by metal arm bands and a trade cloth breechclout. His paint is personal to the warrior. He has also painted his

Chief Gall, the famous Hunkpapa Sioux warrior who led the group which finally cut off from all hope of escape Custer's command of the US 7th Cavalry at the Little Bighorn on 25 June 1876.

horse: lightning marks on the neck, to encourage speed; spots, to represent hail; and a hand mark, indicating an enemy slain in hand-to-hand combat.

G2: Buffalo Calf Road Woman

At the battle of the Rosebud on 17 June 1876, when Gen. Crook's command was severely handled by Crazy Horse, Buffalo Calf Road Woman rescued her brother, Chief Comes-In-Sight. Eight days later this same Cheyenne woman warrior, the wife of Black Coyote, is thought to have fought on horseback at the Greasy Grass. She wears a fine trade cloth dress edged with ribbon and decorated with as many as 300 elk milk-teeth, gathered at the waist by a broad tack belt. Long dentalium earrings, a hair-pipe choker of bone, a trade blanket round the waist and beaded boots complete her costume. The tasselled pommel of her woman's saddle can just be seen, covered by a trade blanket. The bridle is decorated with German silver—as was the harness of many Cheyenne horses, even those of the humblest warriors. She carries a .44 Dragoon Colt. On her cheeks are painted two red circles, representing the rising and setting sun.

G3: Crow scout, US 7th Cavalry

There were six Crow scouts with Custer's force; most of them were probably with Maj. Reno's party at the time of the massacre. Our man wears traditional Crow costume apart from the Army four-button 'sack coat': Custer's scouts were photographed in these coats three years previously. (Full uniform for scouts did not appear until some years after the 1876 war.) His hairstyle is typically Crow: the back is dressed with gum balls, the sides are braided, and the front is swept upwards. From his belt hangs a painted knife case. He wears typical Crow panelled leggings, with a trade cloth breechclout and moccasins. His quirt has a beaded wrist band and an engraved elk antler handle. He is armed with a Springfield carbine.

While the stepped design on these leggings is typical of the Blackfoot, this beadwork pattern was also used by the Sioux, and the fringing suggests that these are, in fact, of Sioux origin.

Bibliography

American Indian Art Magazine

Bancroft-Hunt, *The Indians of the Great Plains* (Orbis)

Blish, *A pictographic History of the Oglala Sioux* (Nebraska)

Burt, *Plains Indians* (Museum of Mankind)

Calf Robe & Hungry Wolf, *Siksika' A Blackfoot Legacy* (Good Medicine)

Conn, *Circles of the World* (Denver Art Museum)

Conn, *Native American Art* (Denver Art Museum)

Conn, *Robes of White Shell and Sunrise* (Denver Art Museum)

Drysdale & Brown, *The Gift of the Sacred Pipe* (Oklahoma)

Ewers, *The Blackfoot: Raiders on the North-Western Plains* (Oklahoma)

Hail, *Hau, Kola* (Haffenreffer Museum of Anthropology)

Hanson, *Metal Weapons, Tools, and Ornaments of the Teton Dakota Indians* (Nebraska)

Hassrick, *The Sioux* (Oklahoma)

Hoebel, *The Cheyennes: Indians of the Great Plains* (Holt, Rinehart & Winston)

Hungry Wolf, *The Blood People* (Harper & Row)

Koch, *Dress Clothing of the Plains Indians* (Oklahoma)

Kroeber, *The Arapaho* (Bison)

Laubin, *Indian Dances of North America* (Oklahoma)

Lowie, *Indians of the Plains* (Bison)

Lowie, *The Crow Indians* (Bison)

Lyford, *Quill and Beadwork of the Western Sioux* (Johnson)

McCracken, *George Catlin and the Old Frontier* (Bonanza)

Mails, *Mystic Warriors of the Plains* (Doubleday)

Marquis, *Wooden Leg* (Bison)

Mayhall, *The Kiowas* (Oklahoma)

Peterson, *Plains Indian Art from Fort Marion* (Univ. of Oklahoma Press)

Powell, *People of the Sacred Mountain* (Harper & Row)

Scherer, *Indians* (Bonanza)

Schmitt and Brown, *Fighting Indians of the West* (Charles Scribner's Sons)

Swanton, *The Indian Tribes of North America* (Smithsonian)

Taylor, *The Warriors of the Plains* (Hamlyn)

The Old West: The Great Chiefs (Time Life)

The Old West: The Indians (Time Life)

The World of the American Indian (National Geographic)

Thomas & Ronnefeldt, *Le Peuple du Premier Homme* (Flammarian)

Thompson, *North American Indian Collection: A Catalogue* (Berne Historical Museum)

Urwin, *The United States Cavalry* (Blandford)

Utley, *The Last Days of the Sioux Nation* (Yale)

Wallace & Hoebel, *The Comanches* (Univ. of Oklahoma Press)

Weist, *History of the Cheyenne People* (Montana)

Wildschut & Ewers, *Crow Indian Beadwork* (Museum of the American Indian Heye Foundation)

Wissler, *North American Indians of the Plains* (American Museum of Natural History)

With Eagle Glance (Museum of the American Indian)

Notes sur les planches en couleur

A Dans les périodes plus reculées, les peaux étaient plus utilisées que les tissus, qui devinrent ultérieurement plus répandus grâce aux marchands blancs. **A1** Membre de la tribu Hidatsa, société de guerriers 'les Chiens de Guerre'. Il a fixé l'extrémité de sa ceinture sur le sol et il combattra sans reculer, conformément au serment de sa société. Les cuissardes et les mocassins sont décorés de rubans; les perles devinrent plus populaires à une période plus tardive, lorsqu'elles furent alles aussi obtenues des marchands blancs. Un scalp pend de sa hache de guerre *Missouri*. **A2** Il porte un costume en peau de bison. Remarquez que les boucliers devinrent plus petits plus tard, avec l'augmentation de l'utilisation du cheval à la guerre. L'arc-lance combiné, ici utilisé comme une arme sérieuse, devint plus tard un object rituel. Un 'sac de médicament' pend du bouclier. **A3** Remarquez la massue de guerre en forme de monture de fusil.

B1 Le costume en peau de daim est décoré de dents d'élan; la coiffe de la société est fabriquée en poils de bison. **B2** Guerrier de la sous-tribu 'Sang' de la nation des Pieds-Noirs; sa tête est décorée de bandes d'hermine. Le mousquet à pierre a un fût coupé d'où pend une pierre à feu. Des objets 'médicaux' sont suspendus à l'épaule gauche: larges graines et plumes de hibou et de faucon. **B3** La capote, les décorations en perles et le fusil se chargeant par la culasse indiquent une période plus tardive. **B4** Coiffe en plumes typique d'un Pied-Noir composée de plumes d'aigle, d'hermine et de crin de cheval. De l'hermine et des perles décorent la 'chemise à queues de belette' et la capote. Il porte un sac à pipe et un 'bâton de cheval' rituel.

C1 Avec sa robe en peau de daim, elle porte—comme beaucoup des autres personnages illustrés—une large ceinture en cuir décorée de clous en laiton. Le berceau du bébé pouvait être suspendu aux épaules de sa mère, à la selle ou à un arbre. **C2** Habillée en tissu de marchand, avec décorations de perles et de coquilles de porcelaines, elle présente les accessoires du fumeur de pipe. **C3, C4** Les enfants favoris étaient habillés dans des versions parfaites et splendidement décorées des vêtements des adultes, avec de nombreuses broderies en perles dans des dessins typiques de la tribu des Pieds-Noirs.

D1 Société Tokala des Sioux—pelisse et queue de renard et arc-lance non bandée. La décoration de poitrine 'hair-pipe' est fabriquée en tubes d'os fins fournis initialement comme ornements de coiffure par les marchands blancs. **D2** Société 'Cante Tinza' des Sioux—coiffe en cornes de bison fendues et en hermine, et 'queues' avec plumes d'aigle, lance à plumes et, pour certains officiers de la société, un sabre capturé ou troqué avec décoration en peau de loutre. **D3** Société 'Kangi Yuha' des Sioux—des corbeaux empaillés et de la peinture noire en sont les caractéristiques particulières principales. **D4** Société 'Miwatani' des Sioux—des plumes de hibou sont utilisées dans les garnitures de flèche; ce personnage tient un bâton 'coup' et une ceinture à fixer au sol, comme le personnage de A1. **D5** Société 'Wiciska' des Sioux—coiffe en plumes d'aigle et en cornes fendues, lance à crochet. **D6** Guerrier Crow, portant un costume de tribu typique et une coiffe en peau d'aigle. **D7** Coiffe en plumes d'aigle et tête d'ours, colliers Crow typiques et—comme sur D6—bouclier décoré de plumes.

E1 Personnage rituel important dans une cérémonie religieuse d'une période reculée. Il a frappé le sol avec les poteaux pour simuler le tonnerre des sabots des bisons. Costume décoratif typique Arapaho de très belle qualité, avec coiffe de plumes d'oie et de cygne, peaux de belette blanche et cornes de bison. **E2** Par contraste, le danseur de la 'danse des fantômes' porte un costume fait partiellement de tissu de marchand, quoique tous les efforts possibles étaient faits pour éviter les articles associés avec l'homme blanc. Les symboles peints sur la chemise et les cuissardes ont une signification religieuse.

F1 Chemise typique de modèle des régions du sud, beaucoup plus soigneusement coupée que les styles du nord, portée avec turban en fourrure, couverture autour de la taille et 'hair-pipe' et décorations en argent d'origine allemande. Le fourreau à arc et le carquois sont en peau de couguar. **F2** Les styles des Kiowa présentaient une coupe plus compliquée des peaux de daim mais des broderies de perles moins d'un travail moins soigneux que les styles des tribus du nord. Remarquez les mocassins hauts, avec des décorations en métal et les décorations de ceinture en argent allemand. **F3** Costume Comanche typique, avec un vieux chapeau 'Hardee' de l'armée américaine des années 1850. **F4** Là aussi, la simplicité du costume des tribus du sud est mise en valeur par des superbes bottes.

G1 L'étendard de cavalerie de la *Troop L, US 7th Cavalry* fut un de ceux capturés au massacre de Custer. Ce guerrier Cheyenne porte une longue coiffe à plumes, ce qui indique non qu'il est un chef mais qu'il est un guerrier respecté. Les articles en cuir brodés de perles sont typiques de l'artisanat Cheyenne du milieu du siècle. Sa peinture de guerre est de conception personnelle. Le cheval est peint avec l'image de la foudre—représentant la vitesse—de la grêle (pois)—représentant la tempête, et d'une main—représentant un ennemi tué en combat corps à corps. **G2** Cette guerrière, femme de Coyote Noir, sauva son frère Chef Vient-en-Vue à la bataille de Rosebud du 17 juin 1875 et à la réputation d'avoir combattu au massacre de Custer une semaine plus tard. Plus de 300 dents d'élan décorent sa robe en tissu de marchand. Même des Cheyenne assez humbles possédaient des décorations de harnais de cheval en argent allemand. **G3** Un des éclaireurs Crow de Custer, avec cuissardes et coiffes Crow typiques et une veste US Army. Comme le personnage de G1, il possède un fouet avec manche lourd, qui faisait aussi office de massue et il porte une carabine Springfield.

Farbtafeln

A In der Frühzeit wurden Tierhäute häufiger verwendet als Stoffe, die erst später über weisse Händler erhältlich wurden. **A1** Mitglied des Hidatsa Stamms, eine Gemeinschaft von 'Dog Soldier' Kriegern. Er hat das Ende seiner Schärpe am Boden befestigt und kämpft, ohne zurückzuweichen, bis zum Ende, getreu dem Eid seiner Gemeinschaft. Die Beinbekleidung und die Mokassins sind mit Stepparbeit dekoriert, die wiederum von Händlern erhältlichen Perlen wurden erst später populär. Von seinem *Missouri* Kriegsbeil hängt ein Skalp. **A2** Dieser Indianer trägt einen Anzug aus Büffelhaut. Man beachte, dass die Schilde später kleiner wurden, als mehr und mehr Pferde im Krieg eingesetzt wurden. Die als Bogen und Lanze verwendbare Waffe, hier als gefährliches Kriegsgerät benutzt, wurde später zu einem rituellen Gegenstand. Am Schild hängt ein 'Medizin-Bündel'. **A3** Man beachte die Kriegskeule in Form eines Gewehrkolbens.

B1 Der Hirschhaut-Anzug ist mit Elchzähnen geschmückt; der zeremonielle Kopfputz besteht aus Büffelhaar. **B2** Krieger des Blut-Unterstamms der Schwarzfuss-Indianer, das Haar mit Hermelinstreifen geschmückt. Die englische Steinschlossmuskete hat einen verkürzten Kolben, an dem ein Feuerzeug hängt. An der linken Schulter hängen 'medizinische' Gegenstände: grosse Samenkeime sowie Eulen- und Falkenfedern. **B3** Deckenmantel, Perlenschmuck und Hinterladergewehr verweisen auf eine spätere Periode. **B4** Typischer Federkopfputz der Schwarzfussindianer mit Adlerfedern, Hermelin und Pferdehaar. Hermelin und Perlen schmücken auch das 'Wieselfell-und Wieselschwanzhemd' und die Decke. Der Indianer trägt eine Pfeifentasche und einen rituellen 'Pferdestock'.

C1 Um ihr Hirschhautkleid trägt diese Indianerin, wie viele andere der hier abgebildeten Vertreter, einen breiten, mit Messingknöpfen verzierten Gürtel. Die Kinderwiege konnte an den Schultern der Mutter angehängt werden oder wurde am Sattel oder an einem Baum befestigt. **C2** Diese Indianerin, in Händlerstoff mit Perlen- und Kaurimuschelschmuck verziert gekleidet, trägt die Gegenstände einer Pfeifenraucherin. **C3, C4** Leiblingskinder wurden mit perfekten, schön dekorierten Mini-Ausführungen der Kleidungsstücke der Erwachsenen bekleidet, mit den reichen Perlenverzierungen in den typischen Mustern der Schwarzfussindianer.

D1 *Tokala*-Gemeinschaft der Sioux-Indianer—Fuchsfell und -schwanz und eine ungespannte Bogenlanze. Der 'hair-pipe' Brustschmuck besteht aus feinen Knochenröhren, die ursprünglich von weissen Händlern als Haarschmuck geliefert wurden. **D2** *Cante Tinza*-Gemeinschaft der Sioux-Indianer—Kopfputz aus geteiltem Büffelhorn und Hermelin und 'Rockschösse' mit Adlerfedern, eine gefederte Lanze und—für einige hohe Kämpfer der Gemeinschaft—ein erbeuteter oder gekaufter Säbel mit Otterfellschmuck. **D3** *Kangi Yuha*-Gemeinschaft der Sioux-Indianer—ausgestopfte Krähen und schwarze Farbe sind die auffälligsten Kennzeichen. **D4** *Miwatani*-Gemeinschaft der Sioux-Indianer—Eulenfedern werden für den Kopfputz und die Pfeilenden verwendet; dieser Indianer trägt einen 'coup-Stock' und eine Schärpe, mit der er sich (wie bei A1) am Boden festnageln kann. **D5** Wiciska-Gemeinschaft der Sioux-Indianer—Kopfputz mit geteiltem Horn und Adlerfedern sowie eine Hakenlanze. **D6** Krähenindianer (Krieger) mit den typischen Stammeskostüm und einem Kopfputz aus Adlerhaut. **D7** Bärenkopf- und Adlerfederkopfputz, typische Halsbänder der Krähenindianer und, wie bei D6, ein mit Federn geschmückter Schild.

E1 Eine wichtige rituelle Gestalt in frühen religiösen Zeremonien; sie schlug mit den Stangen auf den Boden, um den Donner von Büffelhufen anzudeuten. Ein typisches dekoratives Apachenkostüm von hoher Qualität mit einem Kopfputz aus Schwan- und Gänsefedern, weissem Wieselfell und Büffelhörnern. **E2** Im Gegensatz dazu trägt der Geistertänzer ein Kostüm, das zum Teil aus Händlerstoff gemacht ist, obwohl man sich bemühte, die mit dem 'weissen Mann' assoziierten Gegenstände auszuschalten. Die auf Hemd und Beinkleidern aufgemalten Symbole haben rituelle Bedeutung.

F1 Typisches Hemd mit südlichen Mustern, sorgfältiger geschneidert als die Hemden im Norden, mit Fellturban, einer Decke um die Hüften und 'hair-pipe'—sowie deutschem Silberschmuck getragen. Der Bogenbehälter und Köcher sind aus Berglöwenfell. **F2** Der Stil der Kiowa hatte komplizierter geschneiderte Stücke aus Hirschhaut, aber weniger Perlenschmuck als die nördlichen Stämme. Man beachte die hohen Mokassins mit Metallschmuck und den deutschen Silberschmuck auf dem Gürtel. **F3** Typisches Komantschen-Kostüm mit einem alten *US Army Hardee*-Hut der 1850er Jahre. **F4** Hier wird wiederum die Einfachheit des Kostüms der südlichen Stämme von den ausgezeichneten Stiefeln betont.

G1 Der Wimpel des *Troop L, US 7th Cavalry* wurde während der Schlacht mit General Custer erbeutet. Der Cheyenne-Krieger trägt einen langen Federkopfputz, nicht als Zeichen seiner Häuptlingswürde, sondern um sich als bewunderter Krieger auszuschalten. Die perlengeschmückten Rohhautgegenstände sind typisch für die Arbeiten der Cheyenne um die Mitte des Jahrhunderts. Auf dem Pferd sind Blitze aufgemalt (wegen der Geschwindigkeit); die Flecken stellen Hagel und Sturm dar, und die Hand bezeichnet einen im Nahkampf getöteten Feind. **G2** Diese Kriegerin, die Frau des 'Schwarzen Kojoten', rettete ihren Bruder bei der Schlacht am Rosebud am 17. Juni 1876 und soll eine Woche später beim Massaker von General Custers Leuten gekämpft haben. Ihr Kleid aus Händlerstoff ist mit mehr als 300 Elchzähnen verziert. Selbst neidriggestellte Cheyenne-Indianer hatten mit deutschem Silber verziertes Pferdegeschirr. **G3** Einer von Custers Krähenindianer-Scouts mit dem für seinen Stamm typischen Haarstil und Beinkleidern sowie einer *US Army* Jacke. Wie bei G1 eine Peitsche mit einem schweren Griff, der auch als Keule verwendet werden konnte; er trägt einen Springfield Karabiner.